A CAPSULE OF COURAGE:

Memoirs of service & discovery

These memoirs are dedicated in love
to my parents,

Mary Ann MacDonald

&

Michael Joseph Foley

Preface

I do hate forgetting the name of something I have never previously questioned! It's worse than my varicose veins. Oh yes, the odd time the champion speller forgets how to spell an ordinary, everyday word. Getting old doesn't spring up on a person like a daisy. It sneaks in on you when you aren't looking and catches you in mid-sentence so that your mind suddenly and most embarrassingly goes blank – and you say to the air what the hell *was* I just talking about ?

What I am SO glad and happy about is my openness and my lack of prejudice. It may surprise many when I say that all began 60 years ago in my parents' arms – each of them: One educated, brilliant and nurturing, and the other simple, emotional, real, loyal and affectionate. They accepted so many, including visiting family drunks; they were given acceptance, hospitality and love.

Bernie Foley, Clare F's constant companion (now a teetotaler) was one of the occasional guests. These were the only drunks I was familiar with and compassion was the order of the day. Oh there was guy down the street who was poor and then opened a Mom & Pop store and got rich. He couldn't handle the sudden wealth and hit the bottle. His new expensive felt fedora would blow off his head and roll in a snow drift as he staggered along the sidewalk. A neighbor would keep an eye out through a peep hole in the curtains. Shortly thereafter Angus Gillis would be plucked out of a snow bank and dragged home to sleep it off.

There were built-in voluntary safety nets in those days for all people that are non-existent in today's standards. Kindness, so-called caring mostly comes from a government department today. People don't mean to be uncaring; life is running so fast and with two parents working, caring for children and their elderly family members plus running a home, there is just no available time for strangers like there used to be. That's simply reality. We have bigger towns and communities. It's hard to keep up with greeting people on either side of us, let alone others on different streets.

In all my experiences of people, I look to my parents. "My Daddy" was a man of integrity, loyalty, intelligence, wit and charm. He served in the war of 1918, and refused to discuss it.

My first memory as a young child growing up in Antigonish, Nova Scotia was to experience, along with my other six siblings, my dad's return home after shopping for "essentials" for our home. Our dad would *honk, honk, honk* the horn of his old Ford to alert of us of his arrival up our long, dusty road.

As he entered in our doors, we would gather closer to him, and our eyes took on a wide-eyed look of anticipation. Suddenly he would spread his arms out wide, wearing a huge smile, and a *come-and-get-it* look. And we all did... Racing to bulging pockets holding tiny paper bags filled with a brand of candies that we each enjoyed.

The external world was of great significance to our dad. He told me that I needed to be self-aware, as to the make-up of our environment. "Knowledge is the key, and I want my daughters to be educated after elementary school before your two brothers. Men are selfish enough to make it on their own. For one thing, men get jobs that women would not have even a chance to be hired." My dad encouraged me, taught me how to negotiate appropriately in a forum of others without being the cause of hurt feelings in a group. For an orphan at four years of age, he was to me an absolute marvel.

It is little wonder that the influence of the early years at home led me on into social work and a life of service to others, and from there to grow richer from the abundance of knowing myself and knowing others. Truly fear hath no hold of what one can do when bolstered by such unconditional love.

In 1952 I left my small Catholic University of St. Francis Xavier in Nova Scotia for McGill University in Montreal. I arrived in Montreal with my sister who was returning to finish her nursing degree. I was to be in a large class in Social Work at McGill School. My sister and I found a room at Violet Armstrong's home through an R.N. friend of my sister's and it worked out well – twin beds in a good sized room.

Overnight my whole world was turned upside down. I lost my mother to cancer a week before classes were to begin. "We thought you weren't coming," my professor exclaimed. "Now there is only one placement left as no student chose it. It's a Jewish agency. It is take it or leave it," she concluded.

My thoughts were in a whirl. I knew what my parents had told me about Jewish people. To love others was a given for me. My Christian heritage also reminded me that, "Jesus was Jew, and as our Saviour you are to love and honour people of the Jewish faith."

The quandary that I was in at that period in world history was how could I, a Catholic, assist Jewish people who were arriving daily at the brand new Baron de Hirsch Institute in downtown Montreal when they spoke no English and I had no knowledge of Hebrew? These Jewish people arriving by boat had a name: they were called "refugees."

There was one Jewish family in my small University town in Nova Scotia. A million thoughts ran through my head at the time. My graduate year would be a failure. I would not manage to pass my internship, unable to communicate or demonstrate respect and compassion for these new Jewish families as my parents had taught me.

My mother's death haunted me. Now academic failure loomed ahead.

I realized that I had to make the best of it having borrowed $1,000 in cash from McDonald Brothers who had a grocery store on Main Street in Antigonish. They called one of the brothers "Nickel Alex," as he was so frugal he squeaked. Never mind: he trusted in me to return the money, which I did in full at the end of my first year of employment in Montreal at The Red Feather Children's Service Centre.

I needed to take Atwater Avenue which proved a daunting task given the huge traffic jams, loud noisy buses, and people pushing and shoving each other. Once I was given a book of children's tickets by the bus driver and was insulted and became even more insecure. My sister asked her chaplain priest at St. Mary's Catholic Hospital to "help my little sister." I listened quietly and left unimpressed.

I recalled my mother's words, previously offered to me in times of seemingly imminent failure: "All it takes is a capsule of courage," she'd say. I wish I had paid more attention so I would now be better informed. In my grief her words resonated with me and from her wisdom I gathered strength.

Gradually everything became clearer. I was in an enormous city, a French city, and I had little choice but to begin my placement in a Jewish agency, dealing with clients who were victims of war, and whose families had suffered great losses and even death. This privately funded non-profit organization was set up to help Jewish immigrants from anywhere in the world, and especially Israel, enter Canada and be quickly assisted with a broad array of services from birth to death.

I entered this huge building with a trembling heart, not knowing what to expect from staff or clients. My overall feeling was one of total inadequacy. A woman approached me from behind a desk. "You are our new student from McGill. Welcome to Baron de Hirsch. At that moment I knew I had come to the right place. I felt welcomed here. Where would that capsule of courage take me?

I cannot declare that my "English talk" helped my Jewish clients. It was my "non-English" i.e.: my non-verbal language that filled in the blanks. I witnessed rivers of tears, outpourings of sentences that flowed from their mouths. Not a single word did I understand.

I would rise from my chair and pull it close to a wailing mother or a frightened child, quietly taking a damp hand into my own, or offering a shoulder on which to rest. I realize today that I was counseling, in English mind you, mostly married women from the death camps. They were so needy and when I heard Frans P. talk about the war years she reminded me that these sufferings were so deeply embedded in their psyches that the pain never did leave them no matter how long they lived.

I remember hearing about the importance of special candles and of how they were needed for the Sabbath. There was great relief on many a face as one by one people left the building clutching a precious candle in their hands. Slowly and gradually my work expanded. Each senior social worker and staff offered up their experiences to me. I spent a half day at the agency for the academic year; the other half was on course work given by my University professors. My knowledge grew alongside my heart.

No books or visiting professors, including Dr. Wilder Penfield, world famous neuro surgeon for example, could come close to matching what I learned experientially from individuals who had seen or experienced what came to be known as "the Holocaust."

My professional "value" all through that academic year consisted of somehow "speaking the language" of suffering, grieving refugees and simply listening hour after hour to their native tongue. No translation was necessary. Holding a hand, offering a shoulder to collect the tears of others was sufficient. My experiences with each person turned out to be one of the greatest growth opportunities of my life!

I was at the agency for a full academic year. It was love at first sight when I first met my Jewish co-workers. No young inexperienced Caucasian social worker could have asked for a more perfect setting to begin her professional life. They welcomed me with open arms. I learned about the Jewish calendar, the feasts, and oh what wonderful food they would bring and share with me.

I often heard about a Jewish woman named Greta Fisher who was the Jewish Florence Nightingale to so many. Greta, with her deep heart, remarkable communication skills, and eager determination had gone back and forth to Israel time and time again, arriving in Canada with hundreds of exceptional Jewish families. They called her a miracle woman who didn't know the word "no."

Families who came to Canada spoke of Greta often, and that she "moved mountains for us" or "we needed clothes and they were found, or medicine and it was provided." I was told that Greta, with her lovely smile would "try very hard to remind us of God's love us despite what humans have done to hunt, maim or kill." Their eyes would shine, talking about the Sabbath meal, the lighting of the candles and the number of meals that Greta would arrange no matter the circumstance. What Greta did was give back to extraordinary Jewish families who had been treated in a diabolical way for months and even years, a sense of dignity, respect, affirmation, self-worth, faith, and hope for a new future and life in Canada. I thought of my parents, and how these very same values were instilled in us as children, and spilled out beyond our home into our community. My courage was growing!

I came to the Institute one cold January day bundled up in my sister's old brown beaver fur coat that she had given me. It was so bitterly cold waiting for streetcars that tears stung my cheeks and I knew I'd be chilled to the bone by the time I'd arrive. This particular morning, when I burst in grumbling and mumbling to myself, I noticed an unfamiliar pair of boots nearby as I was taking off my own. Just as I looked up, a tall, attractive woman in her 40's with brown, braided hair parted in the middle came around the corner. With a smile that would light up any room, I heard the words, "you must be Loretta." Here, before me stood Greta.

There was no need to shake hands; we were beyond that formality. We embraced warmly. It seemed as if our conversations would never end, or at least I never wanted them to. She was wise, witty, caring and brilliant. I learned "beyond basic" communication skills just watching Greta interact with people whenever she worked in that agency. Her modesty and humility were evident in all of her tasks and responsibilities. I left the Institute at the end of my university year far wiser and enriched beyond words from my involvement in the agency.

In 2000, I achieved a long awaited dream: I boarded a plane for Israel, despite pleadings from others who feared for my safety due to the war images on television at that time. I went, I saw, I marched with others from 105 nations including Canada throughout the streets of Jerusalem. I was amongst thousands of Israelis who were waving, weeping tears of joy for our support in their hour of need.

Looking back on it all as I compile these memoirs I can't help but give thanks for my dear mother and father who poured their love into me, and gave me a hunger to learn and serve. As people of deep faith and pioneers in their respect for men and women alike, they encouraged me to move through life with a capsule of courage. These memoirs are dedicated with love to them, for without them I would never have journeyed on in life so blessed to meet others who faced fears of their own with undying bravery.

Growing Up:

*Early years in
Antigonish, Nova Scotia*

Big Mortals & Little Venials

It all started 40 years ago, when I was a scrawny 7 year old, and in "Big" Grade 1 at Mount St. Bernard College, Antigonish, Nova Scotia. That's where I got my Big Start.

I was in Big Grade 1 at the time. This meant I was 6 months late starting school, having the bad luck to be born in February, and needed to wait an extra year before starting school.

Being of staunch Roman Catholic stock, I had to confess all of my Super Big Sins. These were called Mortals, and according to my class teacher, Reverend Sister Miriam, they could send you *Down Below* as well as put a black indelible mark on your soul here on earth.

I can well remember the state of my soul as a seven year old: I pictured in my mind a heart-shaped soul that was pock-marked with Big Mortals... for frequently: putting spruce gum on Rev. Mother's chair at reading time (her veil would stick to the back); crossed my eyes and thumbed my nose once when Sister Superior passed us Big Mortals in the hallway.

As far as the Little Venials, well I was simply a washout as far as heaven went. My venials were, to be blunt, legion in numbers. Like, take the daily prayer for "our Heathen Brethren in Africa and China." The word "heathen" had a lovely Gaelic lilt to it, and I knew my mother spoke Gaelic and there were no Bad Words in her Gaelic. So I would do sneaky things like squeeze my eyes shut tight and say, "Heh God *please forget* that part about Heathen Brethren."

Another Big Venial I had on my soul had to do with my rejection of large parts of the Credo... "I believe in God the Father," we would all chime together in sing-songy fashion. I could not get it through my head about the part..."who sitteth at the right hand of the Father..." It was my strong view that if God was indeed everything that Mother St. Miriam said, there is no way He'd be sitting around at His Father's right hand doing nothing. I had figured out by then *I* wasn't the only one with 'lots of Big Venials and Mortals on my soul. It was very clear to me that God had His work cut out for Him.
I recall that another Venial Sin, inwardly acknowledged by me to have been committed was the intense burning wish that Patsy Ann Chisholm would put down her all-day sucker during her jump rope turn at recess... so I could sneak a long, lingering lick.

Reverend Mother St. Miriam talked a lot about Impure Thoughts, and of how we were never, never to have them. I finally found out one day by accident. Bold one that I was, I came right out and asked: what is an Impure Thought, Reverent Mother? She turned a deep red, sputtered, pursed her lips, rolled her eyes, and turned to the rest of the class: "WE ALL KNOW what an Impure Thought is, don't we class?" In the dark as much as me, the little traitors dutifully answered, "*Yes, Reverend Mother.*"

Finally, a light came on inside my head when I described to the class, the anatomical differences between girl babies and boy babies. Coming from a family of seven, one does see diapers being changed. I thought Mother St. Miriam would faint during my most descriptive passages. She was speechless at the conclusion to my rather long-winded discourse. I was however, banished to a remote corner of the classroom for the rest of the day.

Time slipped by, and one momentous Friday we were told to prepare our black sooty souls for our First Confession the following day, confession being a requirement for receiving First Communion. I went home with a heavy heart, keenly aware of my sinful state. The following day, all 52 Big Grade One's walked two by two, with eyes downcast, dressed in white dresses and veils from Mount St. Bernard Convent to St. Vivian's Roman Catholic Cathedral, a short distance away.

All went according to plan until we got to the cathedral door. It was no ordinary wooden door; rather the construction was of solid steel as befits the dignity of a cathedral. You walk up five or six steps (cement) before reaching this massive heavy door that clangs shut much like a steel trap.

I wanted to head off my encounter with my Maker in the Black Box (Rev. Mother called it The Confessional) for as long as possible, so I offered to stand and hold the door for each of my classmate to pass into the church. Reverent Mother gave me a beatific smile at this show of generosity, and I remember receiving a pontifical pat on the head accompanied by a "God bless you, dear."

Reverend Mother was the last to enter the church and she turned towards me, beckoning with her index finger to get in front of her. Then, it happened: this terrible, uncontrollable urge to escape. I looked all the way up at this tall, gaunt figure in black nun's robe, with her white "steeple" fluttering up and down before my petrified gaze. I saw Reverent Mother's hand was firmly grasping the heavy brass door handle of the Black Box. Looking to the left and then to the right, I saw no way out.

I was wearing my black brand-new patent leather pointy-toed shoes. Suddenly right foot swung upwards and it neatly connected in the center of Reverend Mother's derriere. There was a gasp, a sharp cry, and I never looked back...

I fairly flew down the cathedral steps, down the Bishop's Hill, and all along the street where the Monument of the Unknown Soldier stands, across the bridge where the little boy drowned and his mother put money in his coffin for the Buddha God, down the Main Street, my heart pounding, my eyes bulging, my coat flying open for all the world to see, my white communion dress in full view.

It seemed to take an eternity before I finally reached the east end of town. The thought of Reverend Mother's battered bottom and my newest Big Mortal spurred me onward.

At last I reached the safety of my mother's arms. We sat together in "the parlor," rocking together in the good *for company only* rocker.

I poured out my troubled soul to my mother
and feel the joy of it still: she heard and
understood my innermost thoughts and fears.

P: S: The following week after, my mother made
a personal visit to the Bishop's Palace to confer
with His Excellency. My mother was permitted
to accompany me into the confessional to
divulge my Big Mortals and Little Venials. It
hardly hurt at all.

Gert: Miss Curiosity

There have been numerous books written in the past as to the impact of birth order. Google informed me in a recent search that over 100 million "visitors" were seeking information on this topic. Free birth order essays and papers were offered too.

My sister Gert was the last to arrive in our family of seven. From the outset, she made her presence known to all and sundry; an appealing voice that was loud and clear. With dark brown hair, large brown eyes and a firm walking pattern, which was more of a stride, her total personality was cemented. Everyone knew of Gert and her warmth and openness, which indicated to us as a family that she was "going places."

I have a firm and authentic image of Gert as a young child as it was my main responsibility to see to her basic needs due to my mother's illness. I would say that it would be difficult to be truly angry with her – yes annoyed perhaps. She was someone without rancor.

It seemed to me that the world was her oyster, and she was determined to conquer it. Our huge asset as a family was, to put it simply, unconditional love. As I have reached an older status as far as years are concerned, it is more remarkable to me than ever what a gift it was for us to receive, and to take with us into adulthood.

Gert was a bundle of energy from the time she leaped out of the bed each morning until she, (and I quote), "hit the sheets," each night.

She was extremely strong and muscular. Of course I have to add that my youngest sister loved sports of all kind, indoors as well as outdoors, even on the coldest day in winter.

My father lacked carpentry skills. He hired a neighbor to "fence her in" as the song went. The built-in fence was not a success. Gert quickly learned after numerous after-school tryouts of stretching her whole body flat on the ground, and sucking in her round stomach. This daily ritual continued for more than a month, and her efforts were finally rewarded by slowly inching her legs under the fence. Gert's escape resembled some middle-aged hula dancer in Hawaii doing her "stuff."

Gert's *sidewalk freedom* proved to be of great success. Gert would sit out front, on a wood block and offer candy "treats" from a Halloween bag to passers-by, who were heading to Saint Martha's Hospital or the train station. Gert loved children above all. Marbles were high on her list of fun games to play outdoors. Her pockets would be sagging due to some fast and furious hand moves she had practiced in advance in her bedroom.

Gert was a pre-teen, and listened regularly to the radio show with The Long Ranger and Tonto. Gert stated with emphasis, "He is a cowboy who helps good people capture the bad guys." Tonto was also a true hero to my sister, because he was an authentic red skin Native American son who was held in high regard. Occasionally my sister would make some unusual *trade-offs* with her game partners outdoors, and I needed to keep a watchful eye in her direction. For example, a fake wood gun slipped into Gert's cache of *prizes* one fall afternoon. Without our knowledge, she was the town champion – "Annie Get Your Fun."

On this particular day, a group of nuns were walking past our front door. I happened to peak out of our living room window, at that very moment. To my horror, Gert pulled out her wooden gun, and wearing a wide smile she exclaimed, "Stick 'em up," to the Sisters in her best Lone Ranger tone.

From inside, I rushed to find a jacket, and opened the front door and walked towards the sidewalk. Naturally I wished to make amends of some sort. I knew for certain that my parents would be wishing the sidewalk would open up and the Sisters would be spared this humiliation.

To my relief, the nuns were smiling widely, extending hands full of chocolate candies all tied up in cellophane and red ribbons. Blushing to the roots of my hair, I walked out onto our grass and said, "Good afternoon Reverend Mothers." We exchanged pleasantries and they continued on to their hospital visit of the sick and elderly patients.

Many years later as a University student I recalled that day. I was in a course by the name of *Behaviour Modification* and learned how reinforcing inappropriate behavior tends to increase this same behavior on an on-going basis. And of course, Gert's behavior was no exception to the rule: my youngest sister sashayed around her own property until she made a shrewd trade with marbles – *round up* on the sidewalk. I heaved a sigh of relief... the gun period was kaput!

We were five girls and Gert was at the end of the line. She was extremely strong and with a build that one would call *husky*. There was no daintiness about her. It was clear to all who knew her that she was determined to confront all odds. Take for example, the ten minute walk to the train station from our home: the minute a train was screaming its entrance, Gert would be *off on a wild tear*, as the station agent later related to me concerning her antics.

Gert's apparel suited her well: they consisted of wide straps on bleached blue overalls with a shirt tail hanging out. "It gives me freedom," she'd shout. Gert's hair was dark and thick. As to a suggestion about the use of a comb, she insisted that running her hands through "did a better job."

Trains with steam engines continued to have a total fascination for her. She'd busy herself at the station, pushing in a parcel or planks of wood that was due to be dropped off at its town destination. It was almost impossible to tell her to go elsewhere. The workers knew that this was her bailiwick, "besides which we get a kick out of her and she is polite," was their response. There were occasions however, that my father was dubious about one of his daughters "hanging around and getting her clean overalls dirty. Why can't she be like her sisters, who are dressed in either Mt. St. Bernard College uniforms or dresses, handmade by Mrs. Willis down the street?" As per my Dad's nature whenever frustrated at such shenanigans, he would raise his hands as if helpless.

Gert's train activities came to a slam-dunk kind of end one day. On a whim, Gert decided she would get to the noon train early. She jumped up on this huge wood – contraption of a wagon. The wheels were large and smooth, due to the oil that leaked from the trains.

Gert was nothing if not determined in any task she took on, including a wagon ten times her size. The oil mix on the wheels of the wagon assisted her in a surprising manner. Her sturdy build, accompanied by some powerful grunts, did the job: There was a loud crackle, and then a booming noise of the train coming down the tracks. Train engineers were sent in numerous directions, aware that there was a wagon half-way down on the tracks. The steam from the engines of the trains roared in agony after being forced to slam on the brakes unexpectedly. As most parents can assume, Gert was banned from daily jaunts to the train station.

I would ask myself many times over and over again, *why is my little sister so inquisitive?* I was in charge of my sister. Being in the middle of a family of seven, I had to constantly keep on the good side of each division.

Life went on as usual: Gert was slightly more attentive to her activities in general. My dad decided to erect a see-through coiled-wire fence. There was a *Don't Fence Me In* look on Gert's face as she gave it a grim perusal. I knew I had my work cut out for me. I did however, become aware of a new Mom and Pop candy store being built a few doors away from my house ...

LADY GAGA ON MAIN STREET

Randy worked for my dad on the Canadian National Railway. Dad was the supervisor of railway tracks and he was adamant that the tracks had to be perfect at all times so no accidents occurred. "He is far from the best man on the rails and has a mean-spirited temperament. I pray every night to keep my patience when Randy sloughs off on the job. Then someone else has to pick up after him," Dad explained. Randy had a conceited way about him, and was unfriendly to the neighbourhood kids. My sister tolerated him but had built up affection for his long-suffering wife whose short name had always been GaGa.

Unabashedly, my saucy sister would stroll down the sidewalk to GaGa's house for a chat. She possibly knew there was a definite chance of receiving at least three white cupcakes smothered in icing so thick "you *hadda'* lick it off," she'd say to a guest, with a loud roar.

Gert came home one day to deliver the neighbourhood's most exciting news in many years. She rushed to be the first one to tell me, words tumbling this way and that way – a result of having six siblings older than she was. Fast and furiously in her fever of excitement, one word after another tumbled from her salivating lips. She exclaimed in her pitch of hilarity, "Large trucks are lined way down . . . as far as the railways tracks!"

There was no necessity to nag my sister from that day on. I did quietly suggest to my sister, as a future "business lady," that she keep away from GaGa's right side. This was due to the reality that if her 225 pound body ever leaned too far over the counter, my dear sister would be squashed down like a plate of pancakes.

I do admit that this new way of life for my sister worked out well for me. In the years that followed, I had to come to the conclusion that with a person of her temperament it was frequently impossible to live with her (I always held my breath to prepare myself for the next high jinx). More often than not, I would find myself feeling lost without that "whirling dervish" young sister.

I may as well tell you that she completed her education with six University degrees, including a doctorate as a Superintendent of Education in the far Northwest Territories. An aboriginal Premier knelt at her feet (almost) for her to come into his newly formed Cabinet and take on four areas of responsibility one at a time, including Minister of Education & Natural Resources.

Eventually my little sister retired. She immediately joined a group of avid and experienced hikers. Even in her late 70's, the mountains would beckon. To this very day, she has no interest whatsoever in ... retirement.

PLAY BALL !

Baseball was a passion of Gert's. My home town of Antigonish had a large park with tennis courts, soccer fields and baseball. To Gert, baseball was *it*. All through the season, I didn't have any concerns when she was tearing around the bases.

An all-girls team had been formed and this brought waves of pleasure to teenagers at Mount St-Bernard College for Women. Gert was popular and practiced long and hard to prove herself. Our whole family heaved a sigh of relief that our youngest sister was shaping up to be responsible as well as involved in a physical activity with her fellow classmates.

Time passed, and as Nova Scotia as an east coast province has a short autumn season it was almost overnight that the leaves appeared with all their glory. It didn't surprise many home owners to find small icicles on their window panes several weeks later. The cool evenings drew us together all the more as a family and we would enjoy the company of one another.

We had a tendency to bond together as a family, and even my dad was a frequent participant when we gathered on Friday evenings. I was often recruited to prepare a huge platter of fudge and oh ... the molasses taffy was another favourite! My mother was a stickler for politeness, decency, and making efforts to live up to our Christian values. We needed to use our *values* and *good conduct* at all times and in all places, at home and in the external environment.

Gert was now a year away from high school at the congregation de Notre Dame that her sisters all attended earlier. "Don't fuss now," she'd say before leaving our home. "I'll be watching my p's and q's" (a frequently used expression that implied appropriate behavior).

I had to admit that during the entire baseball season, all went according to Hoyle. The last game of the season came before we knew it. Gert was beside herself with excitement. She had all her necessary equipment – ball, bat, glove and baseball cap to shield her eyes. Above all, Gert was unable to wipe the smile from her face. "Let the games begin!"

The games began at 1:30 in the parks, which was five minutes from our home. "Take one of your dad's linen handkerchiefs to blow your nose or to use when you are perspiring heavily," my dear mom called out from behind her sewing machine. Gert gave a mighty salute to that sensible suggestion, heading off with her gear in tow and slung over one shoulder.

Gert was broad in the hips and in general appeared to be a dangerous opponent in any game. Some family members came to watch this end of season game. Several of our siblings were loyal and eager to *show off* our whole family. I was no exception.

The following incident took place more than halfway through the tight game. Both teams were going toe to toe for each new inning. No one gave an inch to their opposing rivals. Gert was especially on guard, determined to stand tall and not make an error that would lead to her team's defeat.

I turned away from watching the play for perhaps ten seconds, and when I glanced back again what I saw with horrified eyes was my youngest sister with her blue jeans loose around her knees and holding onto the broken clasp as she raced to first base, then second, and beyond third onto a home run!

Some of my siblings were blushing red as well as purple. The red colour was a result of total embarrassment that a Foley girl was partly undressed, and the purple colour spoke of respect for the runner's concern about a win for the team above a broken jean button.

The family discussed the incident at dinner that night. Pros and cons were expressed and our older sister, now at a dating age, pipped up. She was desperately hoping that a student or professor from St. Francis Xavier University may have captured a photo on his way to the golf links, to bring shame on our family.

Gert stood up for herself in a still triumphant voice: "Mom, I had a serious decision to make and I was the only one to make it. I had to let go of my jeans and instead tear around the bases for my first ever home run." There were several moments when silence sat on every tongue. Suddenly, our mother spoke from the table, "yes dear, you made the right decision to save the game."

THE SEARCH

As a person who felt severe cold at birth despite being clasped tightly in my mother's arms, I dreaded long winters. This particular one seemed and felt like an eternity.

The town had "saved" hundreds of family homes by creating a canal to run through the town that was closest to the ocean. Every year homes were flooded and little could be done.

Our home was fifteen minutes from the Atlantic Ocean. Everyone in town rejoiced to see the miracle of a method for run-off water resulting from overflowing banks. In those days, I frequently felt like a juggler.

My older "almost twin" sister and I were surrogate parents, nursing our bed-ridden mother, comforting our dad, doing the banking, preparing meals, attending classes and looking after our younger siblings. Naturally, I gave little thought to the flood problem. I'd take a deep breath and check on which pot was boiling or whether I remembered to pick up milk.

On one particular occasion, I walked to our backyard for a breather and the sight I saw has stayed with me for a lifetime. It was March and this spring the canal waters were at peak level. The waves were high and enormous blocks of ice were clustered together. Thankfully, the ice blocks were so huge and heavy that they provided refuge for Gert who was sitting in a wood canoe that had gone adrift in the middle of the canal and become lodged. My young adventurous sister had spied the empty canoe and was in a state of rapture that this boat could be hers!

Gert hopscotched from the shoreline over to the next block of ice until she arrived at the spot where the canoe was lodged. For the first minute I was a witness to this, I was unable to move a muscle. I had to act quickly as the currents were travelling with a body of water which had only one goal, and that was to reach the Atlantic Ocean half a mile away. I knew to yell or shout might serve to startle her and she'd lose her bearing.

I uttered prayers when I saw Gert's blocks of ice had started to move. I could see the ice blocks slowly moving toward their final destination: the Atlantic, literally, was at her doorstep!

I sprang into action, looking around in all directions to see any sign of a person who might be outdoors. Seconds were passing and they were ticking to the tune of my own heart. I appeared to be caught between a rock and a hard place.

Gert slid off an ice block now because she herself realized the serious situation that was developing. One look at her ashen face spoke volumes. At least being in a wood canoe was safer than open water, I told myself. I was praying fervently and feeling more desperate as each second passed in a single breath.

I looked upwards for some strange reason. A soldier in full uniform, a lieutenant who seemed to be our angel of mercy appeared on a nearby bridge ahead seemingly out of nowhere. Maybe he was visiting a friend at St. Martha's Hospital, I later told myself. The soldier was holding his walking stick up in the air, which told me that he was of high rank.

"My little sister is going to drown any second now," I screamed, my pitch fairly frantic. "She is in a desperate situation. Please run fast and help me get her out of the boat safely and onto shore!" I stood there watching Gert, desperate as I had nothing to hold out to her to grasp.

In a second the soldier was at my shaking feet. He behaved like someone you see in a movie, calming my sister with soothing and reassuring words. He asked her name and called to her. In a gentle directive voice he said, "Just keep quiet as a little mouse, and I will use my walking stick to pass to you once I get a grip on your hands and shoulders."

It took some smart maneuvers, which he had likely acquired through military training, to keep my sister calm and guide her out of danger. "Look at me and stay perfectly still," he beckoned. Slowly and carefully this angel of mercy jumped from one ice block to another until his stick reached one of Gert's hands, and then the other.

It took great skill to pull a pudgy pre-teen at an awkward angle from a wood canoe to the safety of his strong arms. I was delirious with a mixture of relief and joy!

The officer wrapped Gert into his military jacket, and up the slippery slope he carried her until he reached our front verandah. Gert was pale and shivering from her traumatic experience, and chilled with fright. I pushed our front door open. Gert was unsteady on her feet. Relief was written on her face as well as gratitude toward me and the officer.

I turned my attention to The Rescuer, the one I owed so much to in our dire situation. Within minutes, he had disappeared, literally, into thin air whilst I attended to my sister. I could tell you to this day what he looked like as I stared in wonder while he handled the worst catastrophe of my life in a matter of ten to twelve minutes. Traffic, trucks, children in other yards, and mothers taking clothes off clotheslines had not the slightest inkling of the events that occurred to an ever-adventurous little girl.

IMELDA: MY SISTER-FRIEND OF MY YOUTH

So many times, my sister Imelda and I walked along Harbour Road in Antigonish, Nova Scotia which followed the Atlantic Ocean all the way to our destinations that were unknown at the time, even to us. We had no need for marking time as this was a magic land in our minds, a place where almost anything could happen in this generously green and blue environment.

We carried our precious dollar bills to fivers to the store in search of scrapbooks, and in so doing were pleased to combine two tasks into one: climbing trees, searching for gold (a handful of perfect oak leaves), as well as finding an abandoned wasp's nest left high up in an indigenous tree, accompanied by a bird's nest that fell to our feet in perfect condition.

We would pick wild flowers of all colours and shapes, shouting to one another from a different corner of the hill, admitting simultaneously VIOLETS ARE OUR FAVOURITES. We had to scramble far up into the woods in order to find them as they were traditionally elusive little critters.

It wasn't unusual on our adventures to get our feet wet. No matter; a little bit of dampness on the soles of our feet didn't mean anything at all once we found our prizes. The favourite nestling spots for our violets were under a shady tree, hidden from view. May flowers appear early in the month, especially if the weather behaves, adding golden bursts of sun that spurt between the lacy branches of the cedar trees.

Pink May flowers are so stunningly beautiful, creating a rosy delicate carpet over wide stretches of land. They were not easy to pick. Collapsing in the hand, they wilted so readily it simply was not worth the effort. Instead we sat down very carefully beside our treasure trove and gazed into their little pink faces before we moved on . . . before the sun said good bye to us.

HAPPY DAYS

You will remember I am sure, the 50's television show that many people enjoyed watching, called "Happy Days." I could relate so well to the television show because it was so like my life in Antigonish in so many ways.

I may be biased, but I am going to say it anyway: it was an incredibly wonderful thing to be young and starting out on one's own life journey. The war to end all wars had ended, and there was great hope and optimism that no further great wars would ever happen again.

Soldiers were home from the war (some of them, I need to say, for accuracy's sake) and all kinds of goods and services that had either been non-existent or very rarely seen were now pouring out of every grocery bin. Clothes too, were filling up every store rack with a lot of "decadent" styles and materials such as taffeta, brocades, and velvets.

Imelda and I went to New Glasgow to buy our winter coats, the first since the beginning of the war for us. I was especially thrilled because I usually got all the hand-me-downs!!! Let me tell you that we felt like movie stars when we went to church the following Sunday; the *ooohs* and *ahhhhs* from friends as well as others whom we did not know.

The coats we purchased were in deep emerald green and although they were different in style (mine was loose, and Imelda's was belted), each coat had a matching hood. This hood addition was the work of a famous French designer, and we Foley girls figured we had scored a fashion coup.

My mom approved of our purchases, and we paid for the coats with our own "earned" money. Our daddy was mighty proud of his daughters, and always reminded us that our family name was something we needed to remember and try very hard never to bring shame on our family. However, we knew that if we did make a mistake, our home was the first place to come to for assistance. Our home was a place of guaranteed unconditional love.

Our Little Shangri-La Cabin

One fine day, we were collecting leaves for our science class at Mount St. Bernard Women's College and we wanted to get as many varieties of leaves as possible. We ventured off the beaten path, so to speak, and lo and behold, but what to our wondering eyes did appear ... but a log cabin.

We went in very carefully, calling aloud *hellos* to no one in particular. The cabin had been abandoned for certain, and there had been some furniture in the cabin previously, we deduced, because of the floor marks. We were whispering to each other, as if we were going to see some other human being suddenly appear out of nowhere and ask us what we were doing on this property. Nothing like that at all happened, and so we began our love affair with an abandoned log cabin in the woods, just above the Harbour Road.

Our old nesting instincts that we developed at William's Point began anew. Every week we would take along some items to make the cabin home-like: some seat, tattered curtains for the one window, orange crates that grocery stores sometimes disposed of, and an old rag mat that our mother gave us for the front entrance.

Mother had no qualms whatsoever about our well-being. Children, for the most part, were safe in those days; that would be unheard of today. We were all only twenty minutes away from our own beds. We absolutely adored our little cabin, and we did regard it as our very own as we had resurrected it from oblivion. Nobody gave it to us, nobody used it, and someone had abandoned it.

One day we found a part of an oven, the racks for cooking food. We ingeniously dug a hole with a shovel from our dad's pile of earth near the back basement door. We dragged it along the Harbour Road, taking turns. All the while we could hear the *ping! Ping! Ping!* of the gravel as it hit the steel. We also took along hotdogs, which were extremely popular at the time. Don't ask me how we got the matches to start the outdoor fire but by golly, we had rocks in the fire bed and those hotdogs on the spit. We sat on rubber tires and marveled at our inventiveness ... which proved to be our undoing.

Smoke curls began to unfurl high up in the air, and some local people became concerned. Houses in the area were made of wood, and naturally seeing strange smoke curls extending in an isolated, uninhabited area aroused suspicion. All of a sudden, two farmers broke our quiet reverie.

"What's going on here? What are you children doing with a fire outside, with all kinds of spruce trees all around you?"

We were quick to show our visitors that we had a big pail of water nearby as we always wanted to be ready to put out our open fire. We had carried our pail of water up the hill from the other side of Harbour Road.

"*Never you mind that.* You just *git* on home, and make tracks!" – Which meant shake-a-leg, or else. Devastated, we ran all the way home, and of course left out the pertinent parts in our report with regards to the fire being lit outdoors.

The next day we returned to our little Shangri-La, which was completely burnt to the ground. We let out a terrible cry, of course, as we had put some of our best energies into making the little cabin a place of peace and beauty. At our cabin, we had planted violets, and learned so much about nature, birds, and tiny creatures like squirrels, groundhogs and chipmunks. Strangely enough, it was the perfume of the trees, bushes and flowers that remain with me to this day. There were wild roses, climbing ones at that, whose perfume I found so overwhelming, they required that I sit on a rock for a minute in order to collect myself.

Yes, we lost our last playhouse, but the memory remains to this day.

Winter Thrills: Saint Martha's Hospital Hill

Remember that homemade toboggan, the one with real steering wheels? We were so proud of the toboggan that our dad made for us because it was unique and truly one-of-a-kind. I recall that it was painted with red on it somewhere.

I remember too, that our parents each preached caution to us: to have fun and enjoyment was the whole idea, they reasoned, but the pleasures needed to be tempered with care AND responsibility for ourselves as well as for others.

I recall one particular night when we hauled out the toboggan for some major slides. What a perfect evening it was for some runs on the hills. A full moon guided us along the road up the bottom of Saint Martha's Hospital Hill, which I always imagined as being so far from our home. To my surprise, it was a stone's throw away!

Some of us pulled our toboggans, while others tried to sneak on without getting caught. The culprit was immediately thrown into a snowbank, with dire warnings not to try any further such stunts. It was all in good fun, believe me.

Saint Martha's Hospital Hill was the ultimate in thrills, zooming down into a black icy, slick trail from all of the days' visitors to the hospital. We would go up the Hill as we dared; then we would all pile on, our legs tucked in as tight as we could get them. My sister was usually the leader in front, with her hands on the steering wheel. I can still hear my own screams as we raced down, gaining speed every second. Most of the time, we would turn in at the very bottom, using our feet as a brake along with the steering mechanism in the front that was designed by some ingenious country carpenter.

It was on one of those nights that I have just described that the icy slickness of the Hospital Hill was too much for the steering wheel or our boots to act like brakes. A shaken driver got out of his car and walked towards us, hands waving, and no words coming from his lips. I think he looked down on four pairs of eyes, bulging out of their sockets, and he concluded that our terror was identical to his own!

We were all very subdued on the way back home. We arrived at our front door, tumbled in, faces flushed from the cold and snow flying against us, when we heard our mother's voice from the kitchen telling us that "the hot cocoa is all ready for you." As clever and as typical as most children, we related only PART of the night's excitement to our parents knowing full well that our Saint Martha's Hospital Hill toboggan runs would become only a faint memory if we divulged the WHOLE story.

Growing Others

Social work & service

Welcome to the Pines

1950 ...

When I am in a restaurant, even if it is my last dime, the waitress gets it every time.

Behind the scenes in every posh dining room, history is being made every day.

To read of a brutal murder occurring in the kitchen area around 7 p.m. wouldn't surprise me at all. In fact, I think they actually do. They simply must have developed a marvelous technique of body disposal!

Speaking from experience, I was attacked by a fiery-eyed *sal-ad chef* waving a huge French knife under my nose. I inferred that he had forgotten to put garlic in my guests' garlic salad. The guests had "ordered me" to "rescue" their fresh salad.

Another trick I learned during my serving days was NEVER to question the state of "doneness" of a slice of roast beef. I believed *the well-dones* seemed to fare the best of all. They were simply *rares* with a double dash of gravy.

I am getting ahead of my story. I was a sophomore at St. Francis Xavier University and several of my classmates encouraged me to apply with them for a waitressing job.

The Canadian Pacific Railway Hotel in Digby, Nova Scotia was identical to the Banff Springs Hotel in Alberta with the only difference being that the Digby Pines Hotel was on the Atlantic Ocean instead of at the foot of the Rocky Mountains.

We were accepted and arrived in a flush of giddy, girlish excitement. For me it was, except for a railway trip to Montreal with my older sister, my first time "away" from home for a summer season.

I must say that I found the hotel manager, "Parky" to us, to be unique. He was a former army colonel by the name of James Ramsay Parkinson II who loyally served his country for five years. His army career ended at Armistice.

Some knucklehead bequeathed Parky to the Canadian Pacific Railway. We subsequently inherited him via the Digby Pines Hotel, a summer resort for wealthy Americans.

After we checked into our barrack-style quarters, assembly was called. Parky was waiting in the foyer outside the main dining room. We dutifully lined up for inspection. Parky looked like he was ready for 10 Downing Street. His six foot three inch frame was nattily attired in a three-piece grey pin-striped suit. His black hair had that distinguished bit of grey at the temples and was slicked back with a generous dash of brilliantine. It was impossible to ignore his gleaming teeth because of his Hollywood-style bronzed tanned face. We were briefed on policy with regard to:

1. "Guests: the customer is always right."
2. "Comportment: you have been chosen from hundreds of applications; so act like the ladies that you are."
3. "Dress: not a wrinkle is to be seen in your custom-designed Evangeline uniform."

In actual fact, they were limp, baggy, sickly-green sacks with a cone-shaped cap which we immediately christened dunce hats.

During this ground-breaking first speech, Parky frequently wagged his right index finger for emphasis while nervously tugging at his moustache with his left hand.

"Work hours: from 7:00 a.m. to 11:30 a.m., and 5:30 p.m. to 8:00 p.m." and this was on a good night with no spills. Parky drew himself up to his full height for his next statement.

"If you are remiss in any of your duties, I have the right to fire you on the spot." For this back-breaking schedule, we were paid the princely sum of thirty dollars a month. Yes, you have read correctly and now you know why unions came into being.

Parky's eyes rolled dramatically when he recounted talks of the extra-curricular activities employed by some staff members in previous years. He paused, drew in a deep breath, and half-whispered, "Some of these students had the unmitigated gall to leave the hotel premises with C.P. Railway sheets, towels, and cutlery in their possession. But," he added, "we caught them right there at the railway station and everyone there could hear the clinking and clanking as they turned in their stolen merchandise."

Parky's eyes were like two black smoldering coals at this point, and his eyebrows had reached his hairline. His right hand rose dramatically as he concluded his remarks with this final statement: "Never again will these people be hired by the Canadian Pacific Railway. Think on this, my young employees: they are all black-listed forever."

We all shuddered dutifully, hoping for a merciful conclusion to these verbal salvos.

The final flourish was Parky's demonstration of "The Pines Greeting" which we were to demonstrate to all guests. "Show your teeth, but don't bite 'em." His face broke into a huge grin at his own clever sally at this point once his loud bellows ceased. Alas! His instructions fell on deaf ears as there had been an opening-night party and most of the new employees were still hung over.

We were all marched into the main dining room by the *Maître-de Charles* (pronounced in the French manner) who proceeded with an hour-long lecture concerning the finer art of serving C.P. Railway Hotel clientele.

It appeared that a very big "no no" was for one to permit a hotel guest to eat seafood without fish service. Charles almost swooned before our eyes at the mere thought of such a catastrophe. He looked at our blank stares and finally dismissed us with a quick flick of his fingers. "You all look like the big greenhorns that you actually are," he muttered in his thick accent.

Dorothy, my roommate from St. F.X. University and I ran back to our barracks and fell on our camp cots without even bothering to remove our "precious Evangeline" aprons. I lay there dreaming of my stack of tips that I would have at the end of the season: all the work would be worth it; the new clothes I would buy! My pockets would be a-jingling, I told myself dreamily, when sleep took over my exhausted body.

Dinner time came quickly and we simply bolted down whatever we could find in the cafeteria-style staff dining room. I made friends almost immediately with a jolly Swede who was Chef Number One. He gently steered me to the "right menus" every evening. "You have got to get some meat on those skinny bones of yours," he would say. "*Gee-sus*, don't eat *that*. It's *slops*," he would yell from the counter. We later discovered that ninety-percent of our staff meals were left-overs from two-to-three days previous and had their source from the main kitchen of the hotel.

We all laughed and sometimes poked fun at the hotel establishment and its guests for the simple reason that they put on dreadful airs. My tables were at the very end of the dining room next door to the kitchen swinging door entrance. We were told that my tables were for "transients" who hardly ever showed up. So, unfortunately, I was not very busy at my station but I did, however, have the right-side view of the whole dining room.

There is one particular scenario that would be impossible for me to forget: Charles, in a black tuxedo and matching bow tie, his black crinkly hair tamed down with Brylcreem walked regally into inspect the kitchen activities which was his evening custom. Harriet, a tiny, wispy St. John waitress flustered with having to cope with an influx of hungry guests at her tables was pushing out on the swinging door.

There was a lot of baby clams drawn-in butter floating around for the remainder of that evening.

Fortunately for all, Charles was a gifted tri-linguist, and swore in Czechoslovakian and that helped matters considerably.

We all rallied to Harriet's side later on that evening.

The next few weeks were seemingly endless hours of C.P. Railway Hotel toil. We lacked for any free hours on Sunday as they were included in working days.

Dorothy and I were dressed in our Sunday best to attend an early morning mass service at a nearby Catholic church. Charles, ever the cynic, called out to us with a sneer, "You hurry back here, and say a Hail-y Mary for me."

My pot of gold was very small but in true Horatio Alger fashion I kept hoping for the big break. It came unexpectedly one Saturday evening. Cars lined up for half a mile to dine at The Pines. This meant that my tables would be full. I exuded charm with my "welcome to the Pines" smile to all incoming guests. Parky picked his dining spots every evening: he wanted a full view, especially of all the V.I.P. guests.

Mrs. Parky accompanied her husband on that particular evening. She was a study in contrasts to her husband as she was four feet, ten inches tall, compared to his massive bulk. She twittered and tweaked, fluttering from one place setting to another. She was ubiquitous.

It was accurate to say that my tables were full, all four of them. I was now under the direct gaze of Mr. and Mrs. Parky.

I floated from one table to another, attentive to every small request. Nothing was too difficult for me. "Say the word, and I will respond to you, cherished guests whom I had waited longingly for all summer season, "I repeated to myself over and over. I took orders crisply, noting specific preferences, making side notes for each guest, such as "red lady, big lobster, tan-shirt, heavy male load up, $2.95 extra, prime ribs" and so on, until all orders were taken. I smoothly set down fish service like a veteran.

Suddenly, I received an S.O.S. call from Dorothy, my roommate. She was completely swamped and requested that I "take out" her tray of lobsters-in-the-shell. I nodded in agreement and I walked quickly towards the main kitchen. Everything was proceeding according to my plans. That is, until halfway down the main aisle of the hotel dining room I looked up to see

Parky's hypnotic, ever-bulging eyes riveted on me.

I whispered words of encouragement to myself over and over, such as "no one has power over me unless I give it." My shoulder suddenly, and for no reason other than sheer terror, started to twitch. Slowly one plate of boiled lobster-in-the-shell tumbled off the tray and landed on the floor. There was one medium-sized lobster just at my toe. I kicked it in Parky's direction then sailed past his table, neither looking to the right nor to the left.

Legend has it that Parky had no stomach for lobsters for the duration of the season.

It wasn't all torture, however. Many evenings we would meander down to the beach with a picnic lunch, watch fantastic setting suns all the while exchanging wise cracks with other students, and generally having a great time. Most of the time there was no feeling felt from the hips downward, thanks to the good old C.P.R. exhaustion.

About two weeks before the end of the hotel summer season, we were awakened in our student barracks to shrieks and loud laughter.

It appeared as though some of the hotel (students) staff had thrown caution to the winds and decided on "something stronger" than Coca-Cola for their final beach party. They proceeded to stagger up to the main hotel lobby.

Dozens of us crept from our beds as lights began to go on all over the hotel. Suddenly we spied Parky looming out of the darkness. This mass of corporeal rotundity marched straight towards the revelers who were singing dirty ditties.

I think that what staggered Parky most of all was to discover that *his very own hand-picked Toronto Group*, accustomed to a life of ease and sophistication, were here in the absolute backwoods of the nation and "making damn fools of themselves," to borrow his quote. Beside, Parky wondered to himself, "Whatever will I tell our *dear Maters*?"

With his hand raised dramatically for silence, Parky made the speech of his life. Words such as duty, honour, accountability, and morality spewed forth from his lips in large numbers. Halfway through his speech, one sweet young thing from the University of Toronto blasted forth:

O Parky, dearest Parky, how you are so cute
But Toronto's far away, we don't give a hoot
We've been whooping it up down here at the shore
Johnny Driscoll's just called the bootlegger for more.
So Parky, dear Parky, it's back to beddy bye for you,
But please don't tell Mummsey whatever you do.

Parky, the old Army man that he was, knew when the battle was lost. He hitched up his drooping pajamas, and made a hasty retreat.

Donnie Did It!

My first long-term client for three years was a young man in his early twenties. His parents were highly educated, with two other children: an adopted daughter and a lawyer-son. Donnie's father was a renowned Judge, with high moral values and authenticity in all directions.

Donnie's parents had high expectations for their youngest son: he was a healthy baby in every possible way, walking early and was athletic. Donnie was so very energetic and loved to play ball and compete with his neighbourhood friends, of whom there were many.

Simply put, Donnie's parents assumed this child as a ray of brilliant sunshine and looked forward to his future. Donnie's future looked extremely bright and filled with success. The family travelled, enjoying all their children who were exceptional and gifted.

Donnie was the star: he was brilliant. Handsome in appearance, his wit drew all who knew him to their tables. In short, he was an exceptional, gifted, charismatic six year old, in love with life. There wasn't a moment when Donnie was unwilling to play or laugh and joke around with his family and friends. He learned *instantly*, above his level.

In this household, nothing was amiss: fine dining, with assistance in the home, highly respected individuals were entertained on a regular basis. Unconditional love for each of the children was evidenced in their comfortable environment. This was my honest description of a high-status and responsible family. It would be difficult to meet such charming and welcoming family members and not be impressed with how well they managed to keep a healthy balance of raising their children without evidence of arrogance or conceit. Evident too was a level of compassion and care for one's fellow man within this household.

Then, terrible earth-shattering and unexpected tragedy befell this exceptional family out of the blue. Donnie and his playmates were running around his stunning property, filled with gorgeous trees, flowering bushes along with a play area. Donnie was his usual happy and energetic self, playing out in the deep pockets of perfect hiding places for hide-and-seek. A drunk driver swerved off the main road, and onto the family property. One minute in the life of this family was sublime; they lacked for nothing, especially when it came to true, authentic and unconditional love. The one that followed would be a family catastrophe.

Donnie was an extraordinary brilliant young boy, destined for the high corridors of his father's legal practice – or some high-level career in his choice of many fields. Donnie had been struck on the left side of his head, which meant the reality of serious cerebral brain damage. Jumps in the air, previously so natural for Donnie, now were no longer possible. It was virtually impossible for a young boy of Donnie's abilities to suddenly be capable of accepting vast numbers of incapacities that he previously accepted as normal: running, jumping, doing what he was daily accustomed to doing in play that previously enabled his body to work in perfect harmony.

Every single aspect of the whole family's lives shrunk overnight. Personal adjustments were painful, severe and with ongoing distress to a wonderful family who asked for nothing except to follow their dreams for each individual child. In light of this new reality, there were trips across Canada and from end of the U.S. to another out of a determination to prioritize the highest-level of resources for Donnie, no matter what the financial requirements demanded.

In the 1980's in the northern part of Ontario, Canada, there were certainly many services in medicine by Canada's Universal Health program. However, we had not yet entered the world of technology as it exists today. World-famous Doctor Wilder Penfield addressed my class at McGill University in 1952. As post-grad students, we listened in stunned silence to the world-renowned neurosurgeon as he described surgical procedures on epilepsy. He explained that patients were able to respond to questions Dr. Penfield asked of them.

This was the period that I entered Donnie's life as a seriously disabled, yet still vivacious and charming young man in his early twenties: his energy was astounding and he possessed a *Yes I Can* attitude, reminiscent of President Obama when he entered politics and a push for a possible residential entry after terms as a senator in congress.

At this time, the name of a new assistance program for disabled male or female individuals was called *The March of Dimes*. The basic mission of this new organization in a warehouse-style building with qualified staff of directors and supervisors was to use all necessary equipment available and support individuals by offering paid labour through daily tasks, tailored to the level of their present abilities. Individuals were encouraged by the staff to believe in the possibility of reaching higher levels of achievement as each new task was completed. Positive reinforcements were part of their educational tools.

I was approached by Donnie's parents as soon as they heard through legal circles, that I had established a private practice in the north. Since I was already a mother of five children (one daughter, four sons), I was also an experienced "surrogate" mother, who from age 16 helped my three younger siblings to cope with a 60+ mother diagnosed with breast cancer. My almost twin-sister and I pitched in daily to take over a parental role with a bed-ridden mother, as our dad's work required his absence weekly. No doubt my previous experiential knowledge helped Donnie to accept me personally.

My first image of my new client, whose parents were excited to meet a professional with internment in psychiatric facilities, remains a picture in my mind to this day of a clear-eyed young man with blue eyes, light brown hair and a mixture of sadness and confusion on his countenance.

Donnie was sitting on a wood floor on the second floor of the organization's building. He was literally surrounded, right up to his chin, in a pile of cleaning squares. In a corner, Donnie was completely enveloped in "rags;" mounds of these cloth pieces were on all sides of his body. Donnie's job was to tear these pieces up in order to be put in piles for use in companies requiring such features, for example, in the automotive industry.

In my own parental experience, I had always endeavoured to bend down to the level of the child: *there is a world of difference communicating up rather than down to a child in particular.* His blue eyes looked into mine, because I was sitting on the floor at his level. That meant we were able to communicate both verbally and non-verbally. This "new look" seemed to both surprise him as well as to please him.

Introductions were made and we each quickly stretched a hand to extend warm greetings. I explained to Donnie that his parents had been made aware of the fact that I had established a private full-time practice in Sault Ste. Marie, Ontario (Canada), and was now serving as the first professional Social Worker to do so in that community.

I smiled at Donnie and said, "Donnie, we are going to be spending a lot of time together. Would you like me to be here to help you, and to visit you here often?" A broad smile broke out on Donnie's features. "Yes, yes," was his enthusiastic response. Donnie had a way of holding his head to one side, something to which his parents had made me aware of for physiological reasons: Donnie's severe injuries and serious trauma as a result of the head- on collision Donnie had experienced that day were on the left side of his brain. Donnie clearly enjoyed the reality of being the only employee in this *March of Dimes* organization which focused on severe brain trauma to have, as he put it, *my very own therapist.*

I immediately made up my mind that this "line of work" for a young man in his early twenties, and an IQ of 90, according to his father who had travelled hither and yon to cities all over to find a "place of learning and growth" (to quote the Judge), was far from suitable. Donnie was miserable and wanting to return home after each day.

The *March of Dimes* organization did not take kindly to my recommendation for Donnie. I was a "newcomer," and there was resistance to my belief that this brain-injured young man was capable of high-level learning.

In response to my observation, some in the organization inferred that Donnie was being given higher status due to his family position in the community. I bore the brunt of these statements. In my personal view, a client in need, whether rich or poor, needed appropriate care and compassion. I stated "nothing attempted, nothing gained."

Donnie's father was beaming to learn of my proposal to weekly half hour sessions at my home with a group of other children, and got on the bandwagon. The sessions were arranged on a floor of my home, complete with a bathroom and a side door for privacy purposes. The sessions were set up for young people of virtually all ages, with my secretary serving cookies and hot chocolate at a small kitchen table where each child could be observed in a protected, comfortable environment. Luckily for me, my home had three distinct, visible levels.

Donnie took to his therapy like a duck takes to water... initially. He was smartly dressed in the style of all young men his age, and could walk safely to my office and make friends easily. He had one "problem area" due to his early background: he was raised in wealth and status and gave not a moment's hesitation at any time or to any unknown person, no matter the age, to indicate an "error" in grammar or expression. Accordingly, he was over friendly in personal matters.

Donnie's questions to me, from day one of our professional relationship were *in your face types*: he wanted to know "how much it cost" for my hour of therapy. Indeed, Donnie had come from a well-established and highly respected family in our community. Like yours truly, of Scottish background with parents raising children numbering seven, nothing was ever wasted, and my school teacher mother frequently employed the maxim *a penny saved is a penny earned*. Consequently from that day forward, we agreed that the clock was at one hour of therapy, and any further conversations we had for that day were free of charge. A big grin broke out over Donnie's face at these words, and his eyes glowed with pleasure.

Donnie's overly friendliness regarding personal matters required me to set firm boundaries at the outset of our therapy sessions. Via images on my chalk board depicting individuals in different settings, we practiced *appropriate* behaviours, such as respectful treatment of females his age and above. It was observed by me upon occasion, that he admitted "looking down a girl's dress on the bus," which he had already mastered quickly.

Every adult would have seen Donnie walking somewhere daily in the past: his awkward gate and sloping shoulders gave him away. In a real way, that meant this young man, son of a brilliant Judge, was protected on an ongoing basis. Donnie's sessions with me progressed slowly and carefully. He trusted me as an authentic "therapist" and a motherly figure as well. Any client coming into my office was able to detect a definite scent of food preparation in my kitchen. Teas or coffees were frequently served, and this enabled individuals, couples or families to feel "at home."

Yes, I would acknowledge my degrees on the walls, and I am as human as any other person, making mistakes from time to time. For disabled individuals besides Donnie, I prepared hand books that clearly explained the explanations I was providing verbally. For someone severely brain-damaged as Donnie, on numerous occasions he displayed remarkable intuitive knowledge and sensitivity for others.

Donnie's family lived and moved in high-powered circles at all times. They were a widely travelled, as well as exceptionally gifted family, with an older brother of Donnie's now a respected lawyer, with an adopted sister who brought great joy to the family homestead.

Donnie's family experienced the sudden death of friend from a respected Jewish family who came from Russia years earlier, undoubtedly under heavy financial burdens. They, like so many other Jewish families, worked hard and long to be able to achieve a very high standard of living. The Jewish father was particularly close to Donnie.

Donnie went to the family home at once and cried on the shoulders of others who were present. He was inconsolable as well as uncomprehending; in as far as "a person was here one day and snuffed out the following day."

Donnie was at my door that evening for an unplanned therapy session. He was raised to be financially cautious. His first question, before sitting down was, "Loretta, are you going to charge me for this session?" Maintaining an appropriate demeanour without any change in facial expression, I replied a firm, "No charge."

We talked about the "afterlife" and such questions as "where do we go" and "is there a real heaven."

This was a difficult session for me, too. It helped that I had arranged in the kitchen for copious supplies of Red Rose Tea, crumpets, and chocolate cake with whipped cream on top and on the sides of his plate.

The evening ended in peace and inner harmony: none of us know exactly when we die, except the fact that our physical bodies are relieved forever of any pain or loss that can be felt. As each six month period passed, I spent time on 1) what was possible for Donnie to achieve, and 2) what was not. Donnie adored hockey games and wanted the local team to win all the time ... as a result. He was frequently silenced when he became too rowdy.

An Anglican church in my community built a large addition to its building. This was timely indeed: individuals on welfare and above all, disabled individuals from all walks of life reaped the rewards in no time flat. A beautiful building: modern, fully-equipped to meet every possible need came into being. This decision of a conservative Protestant church was lauded for its fortitude and courage in sending explicit instructions that ALL individuals would be greeted on the Welcome Mat. I met with Donnie's parents and encouraged them to "book an appointment" for Donnie: his father jumped on the idea instantly. Behind the scenes, a majority unfortunately of local naysayers predicted "fires and thunder" to follow in the wake of a "brain-damaged and impulsive young man."

I had dealt with many clients in my private practice, and sometimes booked three months in advance. It was due to the limited numbers of qualified therapists in the far north.

Nothing was further from the truth. Donnie moved into his very own apartment shortly after the new building opened. He was pleased as punch and quite open and friendly with so many other disadvantaged individuals. "They are in the same boat as I am," Donnie explained to me with a considerable degree of pride.

His parents were, at first, somewhat dubious about "Operation Move" as Donnie referred to his new location.

I was able, in the months that followed, to have Donnie meet with a student in Social Services for half of the half hour weekly sessions.

Donnie was her special client, and what a delightful young woman with black ringlets and a smile to melt anyone's heart, let alone Donnie's.

We worked together in my office on appropriate behavioural skills: how Donnie treated his family members (which were excellently); and, external behaviours: how Donnie acted outside of his own intimate "neighbourhood," including the hockey arena, public buses, when floor cleaning at his local college. I had pushed hard for Donnie's special privileges, which worked out well enough that other disabled males and females were also involved in paid jobs.

One crisis did occur at the end of his first year at the new apartment: Donnie set his barbeque on fire, which was a bone of contention to the neighbours from the outset. I did not agree, nor did his parents.

Donnie wanted to be a "big shot" like other disabled residents and luckily, help came quickly. Following that, Donnie had assistance for such tasks. Shortly after my therapy concluded with Donnie, I left the north to move "down south" as they say: Southern Ontario! I received a worried phone call from Donnie's parents one day. "Long distance for Mrs. Loretta Doyle," stated the operator. It turned out that another Loretta Doyle, with similar children's names to some of my own (Brian and Michael) had died. The word spread quickly in Northern communities.

After the operator, the next voice on the phone was from Donnie, who was in tears. "Loretta, I heard you went and died, and it made me feel even sadder than when my Jewish friend Mr. Cohen died."

I, of course, immediately reassured Donnie that we were all hale and hearty as a family. I began an expression of gratitude for the phone call to me from far away, and heard an irritated voice come through on the line. "Well," Donnie said, "I am losing money now on this long distance call, if you are OK." I smiled a big smile to hear those words. There was only *one* Donnie in the universe.

Last Hurrah

Yes, the whole neighbourhood knew about her *rocker routine*: every single night, she was wrapped in her down filled Christmas gift housecoat, smiling down on her dream baby daughter. She seemed to have fallen off a white cloud in the heavens, as it happened so quickly.

I had helped her for some months to consider an adoption: marriage of ten years, and year after year this happily married couple were still childless. Then, following that, they sought out a possibility of giving birth to their own biological infant.

Medical specialists assisted Lindsay through *in vitro fertilization*. It caused a considerable degree of tension, due to Lindsay's husband's Italian, Roman Catholic beliefs.

Normally a serene and calm young woman, in her mid-thirties, Lindsay blew a gasket, as she later expressed to me in my office, "I don't care what religion I am. All I have ever yearned for is to have a warm, loving husband, who is the love of my life. Now," she concluded, "I desperately want to hold a babe in my arms, that I can call my very own."

Lindsay broke down in tears at this part of our session. My own heart was deeply moved, knowing how easy it was for me, at twenty-four and a half years to conceive my first-born child, a little daughter. To this very day, she has brought me nothing except joy and pride.

I asked Lindsay's reluctant husband to come for an individual therapy session. Old habits die hard. He came, and gave me the immediate impression that it was going to be a tough sell.

Whether he was aware of it or not, he was about to face a mother of five children along with a life experience of having to raise three siblings due a dying mother with cancer of the breast as well as the bone.

My calm and certain explanation of an *adoption* decision went something like this: "No one on this earth can predict in advance, the intellect or gender, personality, or size of a fetus in the womb. You are a Christian, to my knowledge, and your faith encourages you as a Believer, to welcome, indeed accept <u>any</u> baby, biologically yours, or an adopted child. Each new baby doesn't enter this world with a tag that says 'Italian' or 'French' or 'English.' We are *expected* to wrap our arms around that tiny human being and devote the next twenty plus years of our lives in unending messages of on-going unconditional love, which is what our Saviour would tell you if He were in my office today."

A dead silence followed for at least five minutes. I folded my hands quietly and presented myself as one who had said every word that had been necessary. Slowly I stood up and Mr. Cudini suddenly jumped up too, as if he were in a daze. He shook my hand with tears in his eyes as he was unable to express his gratitude in words.

Month followed month and Lindsay continued her visits. There was a clear and obvious change this time however: she beamed with happiness, as they waited to hear from the adoption agency.

The big day finally arrived. Lindsay contacted me by phone with these words, "It is a beautiful baby girl! We will name her 'Meghan.'"

With delight, I purchased a lovely baby dress through a children's shop, and received in return a thank you note, with these simple sentences: "Loretta, we can never thank you enough for your help. We will keep this little gift forever so we can tell our little angel she was loved by you even before she came into our own arms."

Lindsay also enclosed an exquisite hand-crafted, framed "Welcome" sign, set in a dark green background. It glows in beauty on my foyer wall to this very day.

The floods in our area finally subsided. Lindsay had requested more on-going therapy sessions, as she informed me, "just in case I may need your assistance and an opening will not be available."

Three weeks passed and Lindsay entered my office with a worried look. I asked her to sit down, and, as we always had done in the past, "work through the current problem, no matter how serious it may appear to be at the outset."

After fifteen minutes of circling around her problem, which she had deemed "impossible" to solve, Lindsay finally got to the "nitty gritty." "Loretta, you must surely be able to remember what happened to our whole world, seven and a half months ago, when I visited my dear auntie, who was so smart and a world traveler. There was a *big* change in her. Her Alzheimer's disease symptoms were evident in her voice, her dragging foot, and an emptiness in her eyes.

 Lindsay continued to speak up about her concerns. "The piles of old quilts she stacks up everywhere make me think she is planning on going somewhere. They say that people with Alzheimer's disease tend to have a sort of *addiction* of some kind. Like, for instance, a son who deeply respected his father, a brilliant and creative man, until Alzheimer's struck him down. He started walking the streets and alleys to pick up sticks then take them back home, putting pile over pile on the green and flowered-filled lawns. With my aunt, all I could see were piles of old soggy and mildew quilts. She stacked them as if she had some intention for them in her mind. Now, I'd agree with anyone who knew of my auntie's brilliance, her travels as a single woman to exotic and fascinating places. I have been struggling to somehow put this puzzle together. My brain could only hold one single thought since Meghan's arrival: her miracle. It's still is like a dream come true that she is here with me."

A strong cup of tea settled us both down in our comfortable chairs in my roomy office. I "broke up" her verbal information into small pieces, much like I was cutting up a pie in my own home for a large family.

We covered a lot of ground at this session: it was necessary for me to question each segment of her authentic true story. I listened to each and every word that Lindsay spoke. All of her explanations were rational, and had touched on sensitive areas in her now failing auntie's life.

I determined that this auntie, despite her personal deterioration, possessed a deep and *unconditional* love for Lindsay. It appeared to me, as I listened to the hundreds of hours each woman had spent in the other's company that the attachment was like steel.

I went over in my brain the possible reason for Lindsay's auntie wishing to send a final and important message to her niece. It appeared that a young family man, a nephew, seemed to be a bully to this precious aunt, and coveted only her money, saved for long periods of time. It was common knowledge that people coming to our own shores "resisted" banking institutions here in our country. Many countries overseas had slid into bankruptcy and thousands would have nothing to fall back on . . . and I thought and put together a logical reason for this dear extraordinary woman to give

Lindsay a final lasting gift . . . *and not speak a single word.* Lindsay joined into the conversation when I brought this unusual "happening" up following her last visit to her auntie's home.

The puzzle seemed to be clearer than ever, in my view. The nephew was banished from the auntie's home, as Lindsay, who was keen to protect her auntie from all dangers of any kind, brought about this wise decision. I am convinced that those who experience a severe drop in their own bodily functions somehow are still *wise* in a sort of "last hurrah." Lindsay and I together recognized that a torn, dirty cardboard box with broken pieces in it wouldn't attract much attention for border guards.

Lindsay aptly recalled how when she last saw her auntie, there was a degree of urgency in her auntie's whole body that she was unable to explain. Lindsay's auntie nevertheless pushed her body forward, retrieving a large battered box, which she passed along with shaking hands to Lindsay. Lindsay told herself she was happy that she had a large trunk in her old car, and no one would take any notice at all. It was not easy for Lindsay to accept the worn, messy, and dirty box as she was a person who was as neat as a pin, as the saying goes.

As it was already dusk, Lindsay told me that hundreds of other shoppers would be "pressing the pedal to the metal" to get across the border and into Canada. She recalled that there was no big time shopping done that day for her. "I was all tied up with thinking of my auntie," she explained.

When it was time to leave her auntie, embraces and tears were exchanged. *Lindsay feared it might be the last of their visits shared.*

The traffic was heavy and the sudden falling rain didn't help to dull Lindsay's sudden feelings of loss. She knew that the Red Cross nurse would be visiting her auntie shortly, and would undoubtedly insist on a trip to the local clinic immediately.

Lindsay and I were about to drink our last sip of tea from my favourite teapot. Lindsay, typically calm and self-contained practically called out her sudden statement. "I have found it," she cried in a triumphant voice. "It was my darling auntie's gift to me . . . her last hurrah!"

Susan

When a little female figure of doll-like size still lives in your memory bank for more than fifty years it is highly unlikely that she will ever leave.

My involvement with Susan R. was professional as I started employment as a young Bachelor of Social Work graduate from McGill University in Montreal. They called it half a Masters in Social Work in those days. I was hired by the Protestant Red Feather agency, and specifically with their Children's Service Centre, an outstanding agency for the needs of all Protestant families in the Montreal area. I can say with all honesty the Protestant community was certainly blessed and I chose this agency over any Catholic one as there were no comparisons: Red Feather was head and shoulders above them all.

Miss Trayes, an agency director I would later meet, was my favourite co-worker, and though unwed she had a depth of understanding of children that I recall to this day. We agreed to disagree on the issue of abortion; today, we would have been in accord.

Susan came from a mixed biological heritage: a Jamaican teenage mother and a 62 year old Russian father who dumped her once he knew she was pregnant. In those days the Afro-American community in Montreal was extremely small. Poverty was rampant and no government funding was available to assist a teenage mother with no education or life skills: illegitimate was the word commonly used to describe such newborns.

I was assigned to the foster home department and Susan was one of my clients. I can still recall my first sight of this little five year old girl. Susan was sitting in a corner of a hallway in a low-cost housing apartment where she lived with her foster mother, a Jamaican woman in her mid-thirties, along with two daughters of around eight and nine years old.

There was no warmth or *life* in this home and clearly there was evidence that Susan was *persona non grata*. I tried to engage her in a conversation and there was no response, not even a murmur. A look of hopelessness shone in her eyes. Her little stick-like legs stretched outwards with no movement in her corner "spot." She continually tugged at her long dark brown curls and seemed to be in a faraway world of her own.

The foster mother's continual response to me over the next several months was that "Susan is so damn dumb that you can't get no word outta' her." At my urgent request, the agency set an appointment for a medical examination. The examination revealed no abnormalities. My bi-monthly visits to Susan's foster home continued and I took careful notes during each visit. I observed that there were no efforts whatsoever made by the foster mom to encourage her daughters to play with Susan when they arrived home from school. In fact, Susan was completely ignored by both the foster mother and her children during my regular visits.

Month followed month and in my work with other families in low-cost housing areas with Afro-American and Jamaican foster parents there was a great deal of positive interaction in these homes. I witnessed a lot of singing and dancing when "Miss Falley" came, as they called me. The emotions expressed by these parents appeared to me after repeated visits to be genuine. They loved to have me come and I couldn't leave without a cup of tea and hot biscuits. Not so with Susan's foster home, and although there was supposed to be a father figure in this home, he was always "away."

As time went on, I noticed a further deterioration in Susan's non-verbal behavior; she was drawn up into a fetal position at some periods during the visits. I suspected that in spite of my supreme efforts to the contrary, Susan's foster mom sensed that I was taking a much deeper interest in Susan than previous workers had done. This probably aroused her suspicions as to what I was up to in terms of Susan's well-being.

Finally I had to act and so I went to my supervisor and explained in great detail what my experience was of Susan's situation in this foster home. I was listened to with respect and

I was given a low-key response. Yes, it was agreed that this was not in any way, shape, or form an ideal foster home for little Susan. Her medical reports gave an *ok* to her physical well-being.

I was told as well that there was no evidence since Susan's early placement in this foster home of physical abuse. Young, newly graduated social workers, I was told, have an idealistic view of the work we inhabit and the reality is we have few enough homes as it is without losing this one. To clinch her argument, my supervisor reminded me that Susan was a mulatto child, whom neither black nor white families wanted in their home in those days.

I had a case load of 60 children in foster care and I had to keep my eyes and ears alert for the other 59 as well. I honestly tried very, very hard to accept the recommendations that my supervisor offered me. I was told, Susan is fine where she is, and this is the best home we can provide for a child of mixed parentage. Well, I could not, and did not do what I was told to do: Susan's little face haunted me.

I returned to my supervisor and asked for a Mental Hygiene Institute (MHI) referral to have Dr. Barza conduct a psychiatric assessment on Susan, and if he so ordered, a psychological assessment as well. I ended my request by saying that after this was complete I would accept their verdict.

To this day, I cannot say enough good things about this remarkable Institution and its staff -- world class, period.

It's not difficult to understand the dilemma my boss was in: concerned about the agency making an unnecessary referral to such a prestigious institution which was besieged on an on-going basis by agencies from far and beyond the borders of Montreal for assessments of a serious nature. At times, life and death situations were involved in terms of incarceration or hospitalization to a mental institution which was like a death-sentence as one couldn't easily escape once sent inside the doors.

Then, of course, there was the mulatto factor...
"Who else would want Susan?" Although it
wasn't mentioned again, my youth of
inexperience hung in the air of her office like a
day with 100% humidity.

My supervisor made a phone call to the agency
director, a remarkable woman named Miss
Trayes. The conversation went back and forth
and I was trying to get the gist of just where
things were regarding Susan's situation and I
was unsuccessful. "I will sleep on it," she told
me. I said to myself, "at least there is hope!" I
said many a prayer that evening.

Bright and early I arrived at work, fully
expecting to meet Miss Trayes as she beat
everyone into work. A big smile spread over
her face as she looked up from her desk into my
inquiring face. "You have permission to write
the report on Susan R. to Dr. Barza," she stated.
Joy spilled over inside of me.
I worked furiously to get the report in, carefully
outlining my regular visits and offering specifics
concerning each observed behavior noted on
each visit. I recollected verbal as well as non-

verbal behavior, noting that for the most part, Susan was mute for most of the time. As well, I gave a clear description of the foster home environment: the foster mother, her children, and how all interacted with Susan. I was hard-pressed to note any positive interaction whatsoever. As someone who visited Susan very frequently, I was witness to the reality that the child was not being encouraged to engage with the foster mother or her children.

I met the foster mother and Susan at the MHI clinic several weeks later. We came together at Dr. Barza's office. The foster mother was in a foul mood and remarked, "All this hoppin' on buses *for nothin'*," spitting out the words to me. Susan was as mute as if she were back in her hall corner at the foster home, only on this day she carried along her rag doll that I had given her on my previous visit.

I sat in close proximity to Susan and slowly moved away so that Dr. B. and his clinical team of psychologists could observe. They were a team that demonstrated a collective warmth and gentleness and were about the business of supporting Susan.

I saw only one look of "change" in Susan's face during the whole time: confusion. I thought that perhaps if I could read this precious little girl's mind at that moment it would likely say, "*Why* is everyone here being so nice to me, letting me touch these bright shiny toys and giving me crayons and pretty picture books to look at. *And why* are they showing me things too, and not once has any one of them taken stuff away from me or shouted or yelled at me?"

I had mixed feelings in my gut as I left the building that day: feelings of inadequacies, the gulf of my inexperience, untired in the field. Maybe I had made things worse for Susan if nothing came of my relentless pursuit of a better way for this powerless child.

In addition, I'd faced some parting words from Susan's foster mom. "This trip was all for *nothin'* and you know *this girl* is nothing,'" she said, as she was heading toward the waiting bus. It was apparent that the foster mother seemed well-aware that she could be losing a pay cheque if indeed Susan were placed in a new foster home.

I continued to question myself over and over the next following weeks as to whether I'd done the right thing for Susan, telling myself I may have made matters worse. I was so very glad to have many other children with whom to work during those weeks of waiting and wondering.

The day finally arrived. I opened Dr. Barza's report as well as the clinical psychologist's assessment and ... OH JOY UNFATHOMED! The well-documented reports of each gave the nod to my request for a change of foster home placement in the best interests of Susan. "Remove this child immediately," was music to my ears. The report described the dire consequences for Susan's emotional and mental development that would occur were she to remain where she was. My heart sang with joy and relief!

The "Home Finding Department" set to work to find the seemingly impossible: a warm, loving permanent foster home for a five year old mulatto girl in Montreal. Dr. B. specifically stated that we needed to find "a warm, maternal mother figure in a home where she will be special. As an only girl, the youngest child, she is to have her own bed and dresser."

On a positive side, I knew one sure fact: all of my other Jamaican/Afro-American home families were models of warmth, humour, accountability and care for their foster children. These families had served our agency well for many years. The "Home Finder" sought their help in considering one more child. All of our efforts were in vain.

It was important to understand that Dr. B. had placed nearly "impossible" home placement recommendations for little Susan. In addition, the mulatto factor could not be ignored as their children would also be in line for possible verbal and physical abuse from both white and black children in their community, as well as their parents. Look back on it all fifty years later; the odds were against our agency and the cultural and racial community in question.

Weeks passed and I grew more concerned about dear Susan who was, I noticed in my foster home visits, sinking deeper into her own little world, retreating all the deeper into that cursed hall corner. Dr. B.'s prediction was coming true right before my eyes.

It was with a heavy heart that I finished my recordings on my 60 caseloads of foster children. The phone rang and I hesitated to answer it, feeling weary and completely drained at that point in time. I picked up the receiver and it was the "Home Finder's Department" with wondrous news: a foster home had been found for Susan!

My heart took a giant leap at this news, and then sank as reality and suspicion set in, questions tumbling out one after the other. I was told Susan's prospective foster home mother looked like the Aunt Jemima pancake box (as indeed such a model existed back in those days) and that her personality matched her looks: warm, gentle but firm. Susan would be the youngest child in the household I was assured, with a teenage sister, a tiny room of her own, complete with a single bed and a dresser. "What's the catch?" I wanted to know, still wrought with suspicion.

I was told that this foster home was in a small, mostly Jamaican community that was not the best area, one that the agency didn't normally consider for a foster home placement. The name was Mackayville. However, this foster home was offered considerably higher standards in many areas such as a spotless home with a foster mom *and* dad for Susan, a teenage sister, as well as a live-in gramma. They were refined church-going people who loved music, were involved in the church choir, and were referred to by many in their community as "good, law-abiding citizens."

All of Dr. B.'s recommendations were met in this foster home and I decided to risk, taking Susan for a first visit. It was like a double-edged sword for us. If these very dark-skinned Jamaicans rejected Susan on the spot, the child would sense it immediately. We would have no other alternative but to return her to a known unhealthy environment. Susan sat quietly with flat affect. One never knew what she was thinking at any given time as we drove out to Mackayville.

We had cautioned the foster family in advance that Susan was not to be fussed over and they were cooperative. I found in exactly what I had hoped for… warm, loving, respectful and very gentle. We stayed for some hours as I needed to get a sense that this, at last, is a real home for Susan. They might not want to adopt her perhaps; however, a permanent foster home was the next best possibility for Susan.

I watched, observed, and yes, I prayed that all would be well for this precious child. Agency officials decided after my report of our visit to the Mackayville foster home that we would make the move rather than do it gradually as was the norm at the time. I made the point to my supervisor that this foster mom had a strong ability to nurture, to be empathetic and yet to be assertive. She was the parent in that home, and thus Susan would be given permission to be a child at all times and in all situations.

The day came for Susan to leave her "hole in the wall." Her tiny suitcase was quickly packed and slammed shut. The foster mother expressed deep resentment and blame, directing her complaints at "the new kid on the block who had recently joined the agency, and who had come in and upset her apple cart."

Needless to say, I made a careful retreat from this foster home and noticed that Susan didn't look back. There were no tears shed by Susan when she was told about going to live with her new foster parents. I do not believe that she could possibly understand what was happening to her. Susan simply took my hand, holding it very tightly until we got in the car.

It took twenty-five minutes to get to the new foster home. Hopefully this will be the final foster home for Susan, I told myself as I drove. With a great sense of relief, we arrived at the new foster home. All of a sudden, Susan's little body lunged at me, pulling my hair, scratching my face, kicking, yelling, and screaming unintelligible phrases. There was an effort made by her to open the car door which was locked even though the vehicle had stopped. I waited and waited for a pause, but none was forthcoming.

I slowly reached out to hold Susan as close to me as I could under the circumstances, understanding this acting out behavior to be perfectly natural and healthy given the situation. I hummed a little tune in my tuneless voice. I patted her rigid back and made rocking motions. Slowly and gradually, Susan's sobs subsided, and the pulling and twisting ceased. Susan's miniature doll-like face cradled onto my shoulder. I wondered how long it had been since she had been held in this manner. We stayed this way for some time.

I felt assured that this family in their new foster home would somehow comprehend what was happening in the agency car at their door. No explanations were needed as I slowly and carefully lifted Susan out of the car. She was relaxed now, almost half-sleeping when I placed her in the arms of her new foster mother who immediately cradled her with great care.

I phoned daily for reports from Susan's foster mom and they were all positive. I made careful note of each piece of information. My first after placement visit was pure joy and I remember it to this day: the change in this little girl in a manner of weeks was simply phenomenal. Susan was running about with hair flying, chasing the family cat and calling out its name. She didn't pay a great deal of attention to me but did make a point to escort me to her room, pointing out the bedspread that had roses on it. It was clear that the family had fallen in love with this little girl as all I could see were beaming faces.

In the months that followed, I continued my follow-up on Susan as she began to blossom like one of the roses on her bedspread.

Susan had come home at last.

Prison for Women: My Internship

The Canadian Federal Prison for Women (P.F.W.), located in Kingston, Ontario, functioned at a maximum security level from 1934 to 2000. Before this date, maximum security female offenders were housed in the female department of the maximum security penitentiary located across the street.

In January 1976, at the suggestion of Dr. Scott, the Chief Federal Psychiatrist of Canada, I began an Internship at the Women's Prison starting in September of that year. Dr. Scott was a very sincere and "real" individual in the true sense of the word and was intensely interested in bringing about innovative changes to archaic institutions. I was about to be one of his "changes." I was informed that I was the first professional therapist in history to accept this daunting task.

Dr. Scott and I were both on the Mental Health Board in Kingston, Ontario at the time. He impressed me as a trained professional and a parent to eight children. He was well- suited for the great burdens that he faced on an everyday basis in his powerful position.

I had volunteered every week for five years to offer my services at the Brockville Psychiatric Hospital where the supposed "incurables" were sent from all over the province. Brockville was referred to by many as "the dumping ground" when I began an internship there. As a result of my professional social work background, I was invited to attend monthly hospital meetings when a Psychiatrist from Ottawa chaired the meetings. Brockville Psychiatric Hospital was already doing great work for the whole province.

During my first year in Brockville, I attended what was referred to as, *Re-motivation Therapy* sessions. Each person was to work with a patient in the institution. Previous therapeutic interventions in the United States demonstrated that patients suffering from mental health diseases lacked social interactions with others.

The goal of Re-motivation Therapy was to reinforce normal conversational behaviours in each psychiatric patient in a relaxed environment for an eight -week treatment. It was *a first*, using this type of therapy. All the patients involved in this new venture were long-term psychiatric patients, as long as ten to eleven years.

Previously all patients in other programs *had no say* – policed. With the initiation of Re-motivational Therapy, positive reinforcement had a reward. Accordingly, a psychiatric patient who was non-communicative, slowly and gradually "opened up" in each new weekly session.

Consequently, there came a day in these therapy sessions of re-motivating the patient wherein fifteen patients eventually left the Psychiatric Hospital in Brockville, with many more to follow. Accordingly, there was a clear requirement for these patients to be provided with appropriate "home-like" apartments in the community.

I was invited to be part of an out-of-town panel named Mental Health Solutions which prepared me for my future at the P.F.W. To the surprise of Dr. Scott and I, our panel was peppered with excellent and well developed questions, all relating to mental health issues. Initially I had not the slightest expectation at the completion of our Brockville panel group that I would be interviewed later for a possible appointment at the penitentiary. To say that I was very familiar with what outside society would term "crazy" would be accurate. Mental health issues have always been of keen interest to me.

My interview with Dr. Scott took place in his old beat-up car, a few parking spots from the Prison for Women's austere and foreboding building. His car had stalled a few minutes prior to meeting and he saw me park close by. When I joined this brilliant physician it was evident to me that his suit had seen better days, and that his shoes were in dire need of a good polish. Undaunted, even by his unkempt finger nails, I had no doubt of his dedication to the needs of others and his desire that women both young and middle-aged, get a better deal than they had in a prison environment.

I confess to being a risk taker by nature, as long as I would be protected by senior administrators when it was required. "Well, Mrs. Doyle, this suggestion of mine will sure as hell be the challenge that you are looking for in your work. You will have your hands full. I will recommend you immediately to the Warden, who has an excellent record, no pun intended."

I told Dr. Scott I would need to think it over with my spouse and five children. I did have experiential knowledge caring for three surrogate siblings in their early teens – with an ill mother. Dr. Scott, in an instant, pounced on this response: "then you can do something *entirely new* with all your *own* children of five, and who are partly grown to maturity!" Dr. Scott clapped his hands, clearly believing that he had discovered the right *new* addition to this effort.

The "something new" proposed by this amazing Canadian physician and psychiatrist was a daunting task indeed: to work with, as well as do individual therapy with women who were incarcerated for the most serious offences on the books. I do recall that my parents encouraged me to always go forward to new heights of achievements. Yet, this *first-ever* task of working with severely damaged and brutalized women forced me to slow down.

Despite Dr. Scott's enthusiastic affirmation that I was the "chosen one" for this task and should not refuse the call, he added, "Now remember this kind of prison break will be one that helps humans face potential change. " At that, I squared my shoulders, and stepped up to the plate.

The Federal Prison for Women (P.F.W.) building itself was a dark, dungeon-style building that was ready for the scrap heap, and it was unfit to house human beings. If memory serves me correctly, there were fewer than one hundred inmates. The maximum security aspect of P.F.W. was as one would expect: ceiling-high steel electronic doors as you entered; security staff with guns at the hip; glass bullet-proofed entrance "cabin." Entry and exit to the facility was via an electric steel gate.

The rooms at the P.F.W. have a smell that lives on in spite of clean-ups; the blood, sweat and tears of thousands of former "inmates," who leave a piece of themselves on the prison walls. The long, winding corridors – damp and moldy – reminded me of The XXX, an old Psychiatric hospital in Eastern Ontario, with underground tunnels used by staff.

Each inmate "lived" in what was essentially a steel locked cage with thick bars. A cafeteria and "theatre" room completed the "house" section of this monstrosity. The exterior of the stone building had thick cement walls completely around it.

The John Howard Society and the Elizabeth Fry Society were external organizations who helped "facilitate extensions" for these incarcerated women. Inmates were allowed to receive phone calls infrequently. One should understand that under no circumstances did these women represent the *real criminal elements* in society, although the overall public attitude was a fantasy-type belief that *"the bad ones were safely behind bars"* to the tune of tens of millions of annual tax dollars.

I found this work both stimulating as well as providing a special skill to the patients in the institution. Subsequently, I was able to demonstrate partially at least, similar conversational behaviours in a maximum security facility to individual women who too were "behind bars," incarcerated for long-term sentences.

Female offenders had virtually no freedom or privacy whatsoever at the P.F.W. When I arranged to set-up my appointments for each incarcerated woman, it was difficult from start to finish. I was told to "always put your back to the wall whenever you have an incarcerated woman come into your office" ... which, was somewhat of a misnomer. My "office" was a closet! I believe that they emptied and threw a desk in, initially with no chair. I am a determined person and so I sat on the desk and wrote my notes... until one day ... I had a chair.

Thankfully my history proved that I was not a shrinking violet by any means, having assumed parental responsibilities in my mid-teens for three younger siblings when our mother was struck down with cancer. My *almost twin sister* and I worked together to manage the household until she left three years later for a nursing career in Montreal. In addition, having raised five children with frequent moves to many cities in both Canada and the United States enabled me to deal with many and various scenarios.

My degrees in human behaviour in the fields of Psychology, Sociology, and Humanities, along with an earlier internship at Baron de Hirsch, a Jewish agency in Montreal prepared me for the tasks at hand. Those returning from the Holocaust were assigned to me. Their pain was painful to see. They spoke only broken English and many had suffered starvation while in concentration camps in Germany and Poland particularly during World War II.

My family, as well as myself experienced some trepidations in taking on this work. Basically, I took to this different responsibility due to the reality that women and children were the ones who suffered and no one with my expertise was there to understand their pain. I was to use the skills and my experiential knowledge I learned from being at different agencies.

Doug Chinnery, "Jack," a Brit with a Cockney accent, was the supportive and kind Warden who added that it would be a challenge no doubt, and though it wouldn't be easy at the prison it would likely be the staff I would have problems with more than the prisoners who weren't pushovers either. I was made aware that the inmates were well respected by the Warden as he didn't always "run by the book," permitting a fellow female inmate to share a cell. His kindness also included pictures to be placed on their walls, and even shower curtains were allowed for the women to have privacy.

Chinnery was true to his word; it was a daunting task mainly to be *accepted* at the prison. I was an *outsider*, in my 40's, with some clout from Dr. Scott *and* the Warden. Chinnery told me he had "no respect at all for those 'Academics' at Queens who never darkened our doors here for some real-life experience with prisoners behind bars… and they fill their heads with all this theoretical stuff." He stated, "at least you are broadening your professional horizons in that you've done considerable work in a Psychiatric facility with individuals as well as group work, under paid supervisor. Now you'll be doing what hasn't been done before in here – family work; and with women who have families and are in on a ten year sentences or more. "

I thanked him for his confidence in me. From that moment on, I had a strong supporter in J. Chinnery, whom I was aware, was sticking his nose out for me. I would say to this day that I was proud to have met Chinnery, a man who agreed to welcome a total stranger in her mid-forties; a parent of five in post-graduate studies, trusting me that I'd not come into his quarters and "mess up the work" on women who were already incarcerated.

I was clear-headed with a professional sense about me enough to know that the knives were out by many other staff members. I was very much resented as *an outsider* that had big-time clout with Warden J. Chinnery. Caught between a rock and a hard place, Warden Chinnery endeavoured to do his best and was under constant pressure as the strong penal Unions had the upper hand permanently and ruled the roost. Mr. Chinnery told me on my first day of working at the P.F.W, "Mrs. Doyle, I tell myself each morning when I enter the P.F.W. doors 'Jack, you're going to have a great day – no matter what – riot threat included. <u>Nothing</u> is going to get me down in here.'"

My supervisor was a Jamaican man who left his family to immigrate to Canada to earn a living as a trained Social Worker in the P.F.W. His credentials protected him from "open" abuse by the custodial staff as he wasn't white <u>and</u> had a foreign accent, both of which were major strikes against him. I believe he was genuinely interested in having a family counsellor assist him in what was an over-loaded case load.

The assistant warden was a man in his mid-forties, a totally closed-minded person, who had a Masters of Social Work degree. The inmates who were close to his age, often those who were arrested when they were caught with drugs, attracted the younger assistants such as him and were given a great deal of attention. He would be seen "leaning in" to listen to titillating stories these pretty women had collected in their former nighttime forays.

On other occasions, the assistant would march around with his leather-bound thesis degree record. I would frequently be forced to listen to his loud-voiced statements of his favourite and repetitive statement, which was, "Gee-sus, Loretta, our best bet today is to cover our asses, keep our noses clean, and above all else, fill out these goddam forms for those nincompoops in Ottawa..: Loretta we've *got to* cover our asses here *all day long*. Remember that." He was right on the money there, in my opinion. Millions of pages of "white paper" (as I called it) flew out of computers that essentially indicated nothing of value or importance to any nerdy human at the other end who received such trash.

I told him I was there to help change the way this prison for women operated, even if it were a small door being opened. An arrangement was made with Queens University, which was already involved in student programs and new community colleges, who were more than prepared to accept such individuals into their ranks. The assistant strongly resisted allowing a group of savvy women from the United States to be granted permission to leave the P.F.W. grounds in order to study. "I have a bloody good reason <u>NOT</u> to let any of these women out of my sight. They are only a few hours from the U.S. border, and with over a 300 million population, they would vanish in the blink of an eye."

Despite the assistant's concerns shortly after the die was cast so that the women were allowed off the grounds of the prison. The women carried books of learning, took cooking courses, and got involved in exercise programs. Health addiction experts were invited "indoors" in order that the inmates could explore the reasons they landed on one of the most revolting and dangerous places on earth.

Access to education and ongoing supports *did* make a difference! Most of the women were there because of poverty, unemployment, poor diets, and negative parental backgrounds. Voltaire, the French Philosopher, is reported to have said, "I own my own words ... until I begin to speak them." It is a truism, in that *some* of these women had their eyes opened to the opportunities that were possible and clearly available to them, even behind bars of steel.

The average custodial employee was as follows: primarily male (as female custodial staff was few and far between, likely 10% of the crew), with a strong macho attitude due to knowing that a strong union existed to back them up.

I refer to the administrative section of the P.F.W. as "The Boys in Blue." Each of the eight boys wore identical suits, and possessed identical thoughts as they shuffled endless reams of bureaucratic paper around their desks and all in threes. Yes, each single act, even if it were to lift a telephone receiver had to be replicated to threes. They were the top administrators of the P.F.W., educated with at least one University degree, and obviously politically oriented and well connected. Each and every day they would huddle in a circle, puffing madly on one cigarette after another.

Conversations went back and forth, and notes would be quickly dashed on note pads. Puffs of cigarettes would float all around their identical navy blue suits, spotless white shirts, nautical ties – and of course, shiny black shoes. I have no doubt that they were delivered to some dark file that *called* it home in some cubby hole and never to feel the touch of a human hand again. I even recall that last sentence I wrote: the bureaucratic shuffle pile was only opened when there was a desperate need to suddenly be forced to "cover our butts." At a certain point in time, The Boys would disperse like birds on a wing, not to be seen for the remainder of the day.

These male administrators' nightly prayers went something like this: "Oh God, let us *please* continue to cover our precious bureaucratic butts. They are, as you already know, all we've got to fall back on." They were what I would call a Motley Crew, giving the impression of *actually being involved* in any rational task. I must be certain to state that some staff members enjoyed titillating stories being shared in whispery tones when it was convenient. A loud guffaw would follow.

There were long coffee breaks during the day at which time these men would huddle together, like football players do, in their see-through glass kiosks. To this day, I can still see their heads almost glued together, with nothing more in their minds other than further distributions of paper chases throughout the vast penal system.

Many, many times during my time behind bar my counselling work was thwarted by custodial staff. I had been warned previously by the warden that the Union resisted the idea of any "newcomers." Time and time again, deliberate delays would occur between the custodial staff and the inmates, those disenfranchised of lower socio-economic strata and powerless women. I'd be castigated for "sitting down with a loonie" or would hear "you're wasting your time with a *low life* like that one..." On occasion they would yell out at me how awful "all these babes in prison *really* are."

Frequently there were deliberate delays put in place by the Boys in Blue that foiled inmates from attending full sessions with me. Inmates on outstanding behavior were in small curtained rooms and the staff would take perhaps half the session time getting them to the therapy as they were sent from one section of the P.F.W. to another.

All the staff with the exception of Mr. Jack Chinnery and my supervisor were total creeps, including the Vice-Warden George Caron. The male custodial officers received a very good salary and regularly did "female checks" and other indecencies. The male staff ran this shop and did "oral exams" and rapes, and got away with it. Every single day of my time at this institution numerous women underwent physical and emotional assault.

One day shortly after I began my family therapy, I entered the main section and faced a steel wall in the form of a gate, like a giant cell. I had to pass through a sensor section similar to an airport before boarding a plane. I walked in confidently having been reassured that a memo had gone out on my presence in the PFW to all staff from Warden Chinnery.

Until the day that I leave this earth, never will I forget the images of a military "Fonzie" soldier in full regalia, including gun at the hip. All of a sudden, the huge custodial officer lunged towards me and grabbed my arm. "Give me your purse," he said in a harsh, rude voice. I replied that I was a professional Social Worker and I was doing counselling work with the inmates. He ignored me and proceeded to step into my face, or almost. I continued to refuse to hand over my purse, and I could see the open defiance in his eyes. A hoarse laugh followed my statement, and in his "Fonzie" mode aggressively shouted, "Hold up your arms!"

I dropped my purse and ran down the corridor that I had taken when I first interviewed in the direction of Mr. Chinnery's office. "Fonzie" was in hot pursuit and I could almost feel his breath practically on my perspiring neck. This was certainly a close encounter of the worst kind!

I threw caution and courtesy to the wind and threw open the door marked 'Warden' and without a knock or a greeting I exclaimed, "Mr. Chinnery, I am sorry to burst in like this, however *this guy* (pointing with my finger) behind me is not treating me in a proper way." Mr. Chinnery looked up in a startled manner, put his pen down, and walked around his desk to plant his six- foot frame in front of "Fonzie" who suddenly appeared tongue-tied. I nodded toward the "Fonzie" creature, still standing like a punk about to strike his target.

I was thinking back to the Warden's words to me in my first interview when he said that each day he tells himself that "today nothing is going to get me down." It crossed my mind that this day was not getting off to a good start for him in any way, shape or form. He rose up from his chair to his full height and beckoned for me to sit down.

"*This* is the professional who is written about on the memo out front stating that she has permission to enter this prison without body checks or personal effect searches, and is here doing a unique job as a family worker with our women. Mrs. D. is to be treated with respect at all times. I repeat, at all times, whether I am here or not. Do you hear me?"

"Fonzie" stood there with his tail between his legs and muttered some kind of message that convinced the Warden that he had been understood. "Fonzie" then nodded to me as if to say that the coast was clear for me to walk safely through the front gates. I held back my desire to smirk at him, knowing my reputation was now "chicken feed" to the rest of the custodial staff. In brief, *I was a marked woman*, to be chased and run into the ground, if at all possible. These insidious creatures meant business. For the life of me, however, at this moment I was fearless. I walked slowly and confidently through clearance with Jack Chinnery at my heels.

It was a very long morning indeed as I saw a number of inmates, including a 58- year old Portuguese woman named Theresa in on a heroin possession charge that put her behind bars for ten years. She was a peasant woman, undoubtedly *taken* by a slick gangster who put out a considerable amount of "shit" as they referred to the "big H" drug, which was found in a compartment of her suitcase at the Toronto airport. With her suitcase filled with hard drugs, she was picked up at Toronto Airport. "No do bad thing," she'd say over and over to me.

Slowly and gradually, with sign language stepping in to the rescue so that Theresa and I could communicate when words on both sides of the desk failed us, we made headway. One day I saw her walk in with a beautiful bird that she had crocheted out of bright red and blue wool. The bird looked as if it were ready to fly away: it was so realistic! Theresa gave me the bird as a token of her appreciation. Regrettably the brightly coloured bird has "disappeared" from my sight... probably in some corner of a moving van many years ago.

Incarcerated women at the Prison for Women ranged in ages from 18 years to late 50 years. The prison population was surely a mixed bag: women from all walks of life and of various socio-economic levels. Their criminal offenses ran the gamut from thefts of goods of $200.00 up to (major) bank embezzlements of hundreds of thousands of dollars, as well as infanticide, murders, and assaults with deadly weapons. Of course, the most popular crime was for drug smuggling, and heroin or cocaine possession, often at the airports. . However the inmates were on a level playing field in the P.F.W., for the most part. I believe I left the P.F.W. "residents" more positively disposed to life than before I stepped behind bars.

For me, it was excruciatingly difficult for most of the eight hour days I spent at the P.F.W. for four months, a woman in her mid-forties with five children at home, and the spouse of a Community College President. This professional "life experience" impacted upon me profoundly. The most irrational scenario of all was to realize that these women were hundreds or even thousands of miles from their own communities. In the case of the Native women, they were even more isolated by language and culture as well as aboriginal status.

French Canadian women were next in line in terms of suffering deep and acute deprivation with respect to language and culture. For the most part "home" to them was "la province de Quebec." I regularly saw a group of five to six women from the Province of Quebec. They were thrilled that I could speak some French with them. These women were to me, at the lowest level mentally, physically and psychologically. Many of the group were from Montreal, and sadly experienced much sexual abuse as their dads fathered offspring through them. "I don't know *nut-ting* different," Lise told me. It was a way of life for these females from dysfunctional families who would be passed around, particularly during drinking bouts.

Strangely enough due to my ability to converse in conversational French, I noticed *shyness*: a need for validation and affirmation. The youngest of the group who had just turned eighteen had used a knife to get a small amount of money from a variety store. She was convicted of a hold-up with a deadly weapon, resulting in her incarceration. She was continuously depressed and I made efforts to encourage her to draw out her pain. She needed to know that she had value.

I had been told by a reliable source that an American student, Susie, who had travelled to foreign countries, was arrested at the Toronto Airport for drug smuggling. The student's sentence was a "full" one: ten years within one year, or her high-powered executive dad would have her *sprung*, as they say. I was secretly delighted. At least one life was hopefully saved a hell-on-earth existence. I admired that she was on my side, so to speak, in regard to education as she insisted, "Give me something worthwhile to do: to read, to learn... so that when I leave this hell-hole I just might have a degree that could give me a job."

Warden Chinnery and his Assistant in Chinnery's private office "thrashed" it out, combing over each rule and regulation, one at a painstaking time in regard to her request for education. I was involved in a plan to permit her to take courses. She was a Queen's University student, highly intelligent as well as under constant and discreet surveillance. The rules were rules, and stiff ones at that, however most of the time Warden Chinnery won the battle.

One day, in a department store at lunch hour I was shocked to hear a cheery voice call out to me: "Hi Loretta, fancy meeting you here!" Susie called. I immediately acknowledged Susie, who was extremely attractive and very bright, and waved my hand with a quick smile. As we stood together, a young woman in her twenties, and a woman in her fifties, I thought to myself: what a waste of this woman's life. Susie could have taught so many young women of both the dangers as well as the consequences of drugs and drug trafficking including the benefits of "being clean" for one's OWN life and the rewards that could be reaped by such an existence.

Bette, a tiny blonde woman in her early twenties, was convicted of trafficking in heroin when she was caught at a Canadian airport with her boyfriend's drug stash in her bag. The scene was like something out of a Hollywood movie: she met a very good-looking guy who was a smooth talker who swept her off her feet and of course promised her she would be wearing diamonds in her underwear before too long. Bette was picked up by an R.C.M.P cover agent and was charged on the spot to suffer a ten year sentence. Bette's boyfriend wasn't charged due to lack of evidence. After her sentence was delivered, this young woman clearly deteriorated before my eyes: most of the hair on her head was pulled out in tufts. She was a first-time offender with no previous record of any kind.

Another older woman, Nancie, guilty of infanticide was given a weekend pass to for good behavior so that she could get married despite having a severe and long sentence. Her three year old son had been hit by her one time too many; the sharp edge of a sofa punctured his tiny skull. She had three years left to serve in her ten year double sentence. Daily she was taunted by other prisoners with shouts such as, *baby killer*. Nancie met a man through the pen pal route and marriage was now being considered. She had an excellent record in the P.F.W and had learned life skills previously absent from her life. "I didn't know any better way to handle kids then what I did. That's how I was raised," she explained.

Warden Chinnery had a long interview with Nancie and gave his permission for Nancie to have a short leave and marry her pen pal. There was a concern by me that another pregnancy would occur . . . and then what? "We have no right to decide reproduction issues," he said. We did see to it that Nancie had a supply of birth control pills through the P.F.W staff when she received her three day marital leave. Warden Chinnery granted her allowance to marry this man as there were no rules against it.

Many native women whom I saw in family counselling sessions were from Northern and Western Canada – mostly from a history of bad cheques ... to the tune of thousands of dollars. They'd bring me their beaded jewelry, their eyes shining with pride and rightfully so, as they were created in a prison all with hands that refused to lie still and play dead. I marveled at their courage. Many other women, almost all in fact, possessed some "gift" to give to others – cooking, hairstyling, sewing (there was a sewing room available), languages, even conversational, excluding high school level grammar.

Kitty, 50 years old, was like a wounded bird: never raising her eyes from the polished surfaces she perpetually polished all day long. She was in my 'office/cupboard' one session and told me how her large family kept ongoing contact with her and loved and respected her dearly. However, Kitty's 250 pound husband beat her continuously and got away with it under the law at the time. Kitty only rebelled, saying "when T started to beat up on my five kids, then something stopped inside of me. I went numb. It was so traumatic for me to see the children were suffering, and without really knowing what I was doing, I bought a rifle through the Eaton's catalogue and shot my husband when he was in a drunken stupor..." "T. 'come' at me with his fists for no reason except he got a rise out of it."

I contacted Kitty's oldest son, a seemingly fine person employed and respected in his community as he had tried repeatedly to secure clemency for his mom as she was suffering from ulcers and stomach problems. Kitty's record at P.F.W. was outstanding in every respect. I wrote a letter in support of her release to Flora

Macdonald., Member of Parliament for Kingston and the islands at the time so that she could be released to a half-way house. Macdonald did nothing at all. The Unions had a lot of clout during this period. If you think of it and put little powerless Kitty on *one side* of the weigh scale and a big fat Union on *the other side*, look and see what you get in "cost/value" at that period in our history of justice. "Abused female syndrome" had not yet entered the medical textbooks as it does today.

Somehow we did make slow but steady progress in our work. Another woman incarcerated for infanticide was only 21 and told me that she was hungry and cold in a freezing apartment in Saskatchewan and had tried to cope with a newborn baby on her own. "He wouldn't stop cryin'…. and I threw him against a wall." She seemed incapable of feeling regret. One question she asked of me caused me to say nothing: "where was *no one* to help me when I needed them?" She definitely raised a good question.

One of the most poignant scenes of my days working at the prison is that of 18- year old Rejeanne, a native woman who was incarcerated for theft over $200.00. It was a long sentence for stealing a warm winter coat.

To me it made no sense whatsoever to place this Western Canadian teenager into a mix of hardened criminals. There were a number of other aboriginal women that were incarcerated for long sentences that tried to "mother" this young woman by way of encouragement in creative arts such as necklace making, knitting, singing, and dancing. I was assigned to work with Rejeanne for two reasons: her fragility and depressed state. Rejeanne demonstrated moods swings and demonstrated a refusal to eat. Finally she went to pieces, striking out and screaming.

One day Warden Chinnery got word to me that he had been forced to place Rejeanne in Solitary on the top floor of the building as this normally placid and peaceful woman "lost her cool and went on a wild rampage." I received permission from him to see Rejeanne who had requested that I visit her, and there was fire in my eyes as I did not give Chinnery an opportunity to revoke his decision. Warden Chinnery requested that I report back as to what I saw, how I found Rejeanne, and what my recommendations were regarding her: to stay in polity or to be released.

I could hear the warning calls as I followed the custodial male staff out of the "regular" section and on to "solitary." I had been warned to be "careful of this little demon" by the staff. I had no fear as I approached solitary, accompanied by this custodial member as *he knew that I knew* he'd better watch his p's and q's with me at all times! I was in the driver's seat, going on a mission for Warden Chinnery as solitary confinements were only taken under very serious consideration where violence was a high probability.

There was a lot of sadness expressed by the other inmates despite their personal safety concerns. Many suggested that I might be of help. However, some said, "Be careful, she's dangerous now. She's a wild cat when she gets her claws in you." For some reason, perhaps having five children of my own, I had an intuitive sense of what it must be like to be in this nightmare of a building

I remember the day that Mr. Chinnery ordered me to "prepare myself" for the trip up a flight of enormous stone stairs – like the Hunchback of

Notre Dame's quarters in the famous film with Charles Laughton and a young Maureen O'Hara . At the top of the flight, I looked downwards to see a shocking sight: it was a Canadian military officer in full battle gear. To my horror, I saw below that this military soldier with a gun at his hip was the same "Fonzie "custodial staff who had accosted me as soon as Warden Chinnery's back was turned on the first day of my internship! To make matters worse, he was, at 6- feet 5 inches tall, heads above my 5 foot 3 inches stature, putting me at a disadvantage to say the least.

Suddenly my own dear departed mother's face came into view: a young woman in her early twenties, with a teacher's diploma in hand, venturing to the western parts of Canada and to some of the coldest temperatures, -55-60 degrees. The 1914-1918 war had ended, and German immigrants poured into barren parts of our country of Canada. It was what we would call today in the jargon, "a good deal all around," with talented European citizens who were weary and desperate for a new life.

In my mind, right then and there in this moment of fear as I walked behind this bully wearing size 22-plus military boots, I opened a "capsule of courage:" that of my own dear mother who so often reminded me of keeping myself safe and confident.

As I walked up those stone stairs to the top of the institution, there was Rejeanne on the bare floor of the prison with a dirty mattress flung against the wall. A bucket stood in the far corner. She was wearing a ragged dress with Native edges. There were no blankets or sheets as these were forbidden at the prison for fear of attempts of suicide.

The terror in her tiny face was that of a waif out of a Charles Dickens' novel and I experienced a jolt of anger which I could not show outwardly. She shrank into her corner and turned away from me, when the "Fonzie" in military garb approached the cell. I whirled around and said in a loud and stern voice, "*you* are no longer charge here. My task is to assist this young teenager out of the prison she is in at *this* very moment. My work and training will be prevented until you 'back off NOW' AND STAND IN THE HALLWAY OF THIS PRISON. If you do not obey my instructions from Warden Chinnery, I will report you."

Slightly mollified, "Fonzie" straightened out his six- six frame and turned his head toward the wall. At this point, Rejeanne crawled over to where I was now seated on the floor behind the bars that separated us. My heart beat in my chest as I had a fainting experience, realizing that there had previously been thousands of others on these blood-stained floors before me.

Rejeanne had deep sadness in her eyes and the smell of terror in the room. There was a pail in the corner of the cell and that was all. The guard left us, and I dropped to the floor on the outside of her locked solitary cell. I said nothing at first, and we sat and watched each other warily.

Another few minutes passed and the silence ensued. What I viewed from my vantage point, was the child-like woman of a slight build, powerless. I thought of what I would do if suddenly the cell would evaporate. Then she would be just a scared, young woman!

I slowly and quietly leaned over so slightly toward Rejeanne. There was no change in our situation... and yet there was. Her eyes, for one thing, seemed to have lost some of their fear. I had read somewhere that a rat who is cornered is a lot more dangerous and volatile than one who is running around ... and so are humans.

Rejeanne appeared to have sensed that I had come *in peace*, so to speak. I said her name very softly. She moved closer to my spot. I very, very quietly put my right hand inside the cell. With no possibility of a weapon on her person, I had no real sense of being in danger. I possessed no key to unlock the cell door, and she knew it.

My conversation with her was to tell her that I cared about her; that she was in my thoughts, and that others were hoping that she would be released soon from solitary. My advice to her was to be quiet and polite when the custodial officers came around to check on her, and that I too would let the Warden know that her behavior was appropriate.

Rejeanne lifted her two trembling hands up to mine and squeezed mine. One does not forget such a touch. Within an hour's time, Warden Chinnery released Rejeanne and upon my recommendation, she returned home to her First Nations' Village.

My last professional involvement at the Prison for Women began on a regular day. Actually, if memory serves me correctly, I was treated decently at the entrance wicket... no hassle, no sweat, no verbal taunts – thanks to Warden Chinnery.

Like any other punitive institution, the P.F.W. had a "miraculous" grapevine, when one considers the locked cells and crushing custodial surveillance at all times and in a 24-hour period.

I cannot recall which person leaned over with a whispered statement, "XXX has told our 'group'..." her sentence trailed. The 'group' consisted of aboriginal incarcerated women, French Canadian women, and others from foreign countries such as Spain and the United States. The information whispered to me was probably by someone designated to speak on the group's behalf. The French Canadian group was frantically trying to get word out to me that XXX planned to slit her throat sometime later on that very day.

I had a quick decision to make: run the risk of being completely alienated by the P.F.W. because I "squealed" on one of their own, *or* breach confidentiality to hopefully save a life. I had a strong suspicion that the young woman was under twenty years old. In other words, she was capable of killing herself. Besides her sentence would be a long one, increasing the likelihood of eventual suicide.

I immediately reported this important information to my male supervisor from Jamaica (who was continually treated disrespectfully due to his dark skin). He put other staff on alert for the remainder of the days. XXX was under surveillance constantly.

There was an air of tension that I felt amongst the staff. I considered the real possibility of a depressed 18 year old that killed herself despite armed custodial staff would not go well with the P.F.W. population as well as the Canadian population in general. After all is said and done, this *was* a Federal Institution with every possible piece of equipment, support staff, plus instant cooperation and assistance in a major prison disaster.

On this day in the prison for women at 3:30 p.m., my supervisor rushed up to me as I sat waiting in my tiny cubicle. All I could see was the white of his eyes as he said, "XXX. She slit her throat halfway, but her life isn't in danger. She is now in I.C.U." With tears in his eyes my Supervisor looked at me and said, "I give you a merciful thank you. A young life has been saved because of your quick response." Without even thinking, I hugged him in plain sight of all, thankful that he believed me in the first place and had taken subsequent appropriate actions so that a young woman's life was saved.

The fact that XXX managed to get her hands on half of a Gillette razor was the mystery of the P.F.W. considering that she was searched _and_ was under unceasing surveillance. It was my belief and mine alone, never expressed until this very day, that another person feeling XXX's pain, loss and desperation day after day with a ten year sentence hanging over her, hid it for her and saw that she got it at the right moment of her own choosing.

After my supervisor and I joyfully embraced, the final "rub" set in on me as the custodial staff whispered to one another and proceeded to pour on the heat. I had my purse and briefcase and walked confidently toward the steel-walled gates. I pressed the button for the cell door to rise so I could leave, and nothing happened. I looked over and I could see out of the corner of my eye that the Boys in Blue were in the glass booth and were having one hell of a good laugh at my expense. I could plainly see that I was being mocked and discounted by two other custodial staff that pointed at me and embraced each other.

I stood and waited. Time passed and there was no chair on which to sit. This had been a long, tension-filled day. I decided that somehow I couldn't allow my inner anger and frustration to show. There was no one else I could get help from as my supervisor and I had waited to get the all clear report on the inmate and had parted, and there was no phone either for "outside or inside" where I was located in the building. I was completely shut off and at the mercy of their childish antics. I had no control whatsoever and they knew it.

Finally I leaned against the side wall as opposed to the steel floor-to-ceiling doors. As always, I never went far without a book of some sort. That day I had a textbook on behaviour modification. Skinner was big in those days. For some reason, it had an attractive and sensual cover with male and female figures. I slowly put my briefcase on the floor, opened it, and pulled out my book, quickly snapping the lock on my briefcase.

The next thirty minutes with my reader glasses on, I poured over the book and displayed intense interest as best I could. I laughed heartily at least on every page, and sometimes it was only a mild chuckle. I took my pen out of my purse and awkwardly underlined certain passages, being sure to hold the book facing the Boys in Blue as often as I possibly could without making it so obvious that they would catch on to what I was attempting to do. Sometimes I would go back a page or two and reread a few lines, laughing again.

Finally the Boys grew both bored and confused. I wasn't screaming invectives, nor was I threatening them and they were plainly discouraged by my dismissal of them. Upon the opening of the gate, I threw my keys in and smiled a victorious smile on their *ta-da* faces and went out the gate, inwardly thanking my lucky stars. My first in Canada family counselling role at the Prison for Women was almost completed. I thought: If only the world knew! Better to wait, I said. *And here I am telling it like it was.*

The best title for my story of working with incarcerated women in a maximum security facility might very well be *My Time Behind Bars!* I have described some very tragic cases and occasionally, there was the odd flicker of humour that I experienced.

One day I was making a bit of headway with one of the most difficult prisoners in terms of her total withdrawal, and I failed to notice the time. It was lunch time and the usual ritual was for all staff going for lunch would basically leave at the same time. It made sense in that all prisoners had to be in particular spots too at specific times.

I looked up in amazement to find that the staff in their large square/high fenced-in secretarial section had locked up, leaving me with my coats and boots but no way out. Mr. Chinnery was nowhere to be seen and that was probably the reason for the Boys horsing around with me. I was determined to succeed in my efforts to somehow "make my way" out of this dilemma.

As I was half seated at one of the tall desks I suddenly noticed that there was the lower section of a large mail chute just above it. It felt a piece of shining wood, similar to a "run." Maybe, just maybe I could climb down the chute... carefully. I poked my head up, just long enough to see where it "ended." It wasn't high and neither was it all that slippery. I realized I'd need to straddle in order to make any upward gains. Just maybe, I could climb up the chute very, very carefully.

I decided to roll up my coat and push it up the chute first, followed by my boots.   I don't think the Boys even heard or noticed the drop of my outerwear. Besides which, these total jerks suffered severely from inattention and no doubt their empty little skulls were busy taunting some other unsuspecting soul, perhaps from the John Howard Society.

I felt like Archimedes sitting in his bathtub pondering a heavy duty problem. With my gear safely ahead of me, the next "push" forward was my own body.   I realized I would need to straddle, in order to make any upward gains. I recall wearing a midi-length wool skirt that came to my ankles. Slacks would have been better, no doubt about it, I thought to myself. It was a Murphy's Law type of day. I was up at 6 a.m. to make sure that my children were organized and "out" for school and there was no possibilities of food or drink until I left at 5:30 p.m. My gnawing empty stomach began to chortle empty noises and pushed me forward toward my exit goal. Slowly and carefully I pulled myself up on the desk top after carefully wrapping my midi skirt tightly around my legs as best I could so as not to hitch my skirt up too high.

With my head bent back as far as possible on the stoop of the chute, I closed my eyes and held on to my skirt and climbed up the mail chute slide, landing with such a bang on the hard floor that I did manage to get their attention. I picked myself up off the floor, feeling for broken bones. Satisfied that I was still in one piece, I let out a non-verbal shout and raised my fist in the air. In 60 seconds flat, I leaned over and stretching out to retrieve my warm coat, boots, I put them on, gripping my purse in my hot little hand for the final exit. Bravo! The Boys in Blue had no time to render any guffaws.

Of course I had felt the brunt of the little head game played at the steel gate, finding the Boys "busy" at ... nothing! The gates swung open for me and as I set my keys to this "Kingdom of Evil" down, my hand was grabbed hard and squeezed. I attempted to pull away to no avail. I looked up and straight into "Fonzie's" face. "I have a husband who loves me and my children very much. He will run you to the ends of the earth when I tell him you are holding me here against my will." He let me go immediately. I couldn't figure out how my words made such a difference. I was angry and hungry and perhaps I sounded more convincing than I realized at the time. Out the gate I went for a late lunch. I wisely did not rub it in that they had played a childish game of chicken and lost. My lunch tasted especially good that day!

I had very positive reactions from the women with regard to therapy sessions in our little "pigmy" cupboards in which we met. They appeared to me to manifest authentic gratitude to be "present" here in prison and have another human being with them, especially an experienced mother of children. Along with sharing theoretical knowledge with the women, they were starved for new information and enjoyed conversing. Together we were able to gain some insight into how they were imprisoned in the first place, along with some family planning once they were released. For me, the most rewarding time I spent was with the married women's group along and single parents.

On my last day of internship, Mr. Chinnery arranged for a tea and coffee good-bye party for me and gave a little speech as to express his appreciation for the significant contributions I had made during my stay. Some of the "good behavior" P.F.W. women were allowed to join us along with select staff.

The Warden stated this party was a *first* in the prison's history. He commended me for a job well done in a difficult family worker's role for the *first* time ever. The therapy sessions were a big help to all those women who requested a session or more on their own. That meant trust on both sides of the aisle. I waved my hands upwards to the group with a big smile and thanked them.

Helen, my Masters of Social Work Carleton University Supervisor made one visit to the prison. Her teeth were clenched when she related to me her experience at the main entrance and "Fonzie's" unwelcoming treatment of her. Her response was, "never again will Carleton University permit a second encounter with these guys!"

To the best of my knowledge no other Masters of Social Work students stepped up to the base at the Federal Prison for Women.

The Federal Prison for Women in Kingston was eventually closed following a number of controversial incidents. LSD was administered to inmates at the prison as part of tests that are considered today to be ethically dubious. In 1994, a riot broke out at the prison, resulting in Justice Louise Arbour, then of the Ontario Court of Appeal, heading up what became known as the Commission of Inquiry into certain events at the prison for women in Kingston which found that the treatment of prisoners at the facility had been "*cruel, inhumane and degrading*."

Growing Richer

Life lessons along the way

Houses I Have Known

Each home that we have lived in over the past twenty years has certain endearing qualities and characteristics that have stayed with me over the years. I believe that it is important for family reasons to share some of these memories with my reader.

We had a "thing" about attics in the early part of our marriage. We lived in quite a few. <u>The Peterboro House</u> was one of these; it had a pointed roof and we were at the top of the roof. Yes, it is true that one side of my head had a caved-in look after six months in these quarters.

I can imagine the two of us to this very day sitting down at our brand new arborite kitchen table, conversing. The toasts would pop ... *boing* ... oh I forgot the salt for the eggs ... *boing* again ... there's the timer going off for the muffins ... *bam* ... *crunch*. No dear, there is only internal bleeding in case you think the neighbours will think of assault and battery charges.

This abode had no private entrance and our bedroom had no door. You have no idea how disturbing it is to be partially undressed only to find yourself gazing at Mr. or Mrs. Lasky, or worse, their bratty, twelve year old twins. They would come to the top of the stairs, peer in at us and loudly exclaim, "Hey how come you two are in the same bed? Our parents have two beds in their room."

The Avon House in Montreal West, named after the river Avon in England, was in a class all its' own. It was actually our first place and cost $85.00 a month (furnished). The furnishings consisted of a saggy mattress with springs sticking out, a mildewed-moth-eaten grey living room carpet with a matching sofa. Pussy willows draped in bowls and pitchers were expected to cover a multitude of sins.

The living room ceiling was built for a dwarf. We walked around semi-stooped the whole evening when we came home from work. Sound exciting? I have saved the best for last. The kitchen was absolutely unique. I have never, thank goodness, encountered a similar model since then.

The "kitchen" was actually a hallway between the living room and our bedroom. The pots, pans, utensils, and dishes were spread out on a tiny sideboard when we first looked at the apartment. Everything had a cluttered, piled-on-high look about it. It was only after we moved in that I realized why: camouflage, that's why! "Chuckle, chuckle," trilled Mrs. Avon. "It's such a lark doing dishes in the *bath tub*. All of our young honeymooners simply adore it."

Oh yes, it was an absolute barrel of laughs. I can remember it still: soaking in a hot bath after returning from the Children's Centre Agency. Suddenly I came face-to-face with floating orange peelings or toast crusts inching their way into the tub corners.

When it comes to stand-outs, <u>The Bee House</u> was no slouch either. We lived in a basement apartment. My 18-month old daughter and I used to go out together to the back lawn. I dragged the playpen out with one hand and she was carried out in my arms in the other. This was so that I could hang out the laundry on the clothesline. M. Grenier, our landlord, lived next door. He was a frustrated farmer; his sidelines consisted of our apartment building and ... bees. He had a thriving honey business going and we daily faced stacks of beehives a few feet away.

I have always kept a comfortable distance between myself and all bees. M. Grenier's beehives didn't change that decision. "N'ayez pas peur Madame," he'd shout to me above the swarm of buzzing bees. "Les abeilles, ells sont tres fines," he added as he adjusted his heavy net jungle gym helmet and tugged at his thick leather elbow length gloves. It must have been hot that summer in those heavy corduroy pants and high leather boots.

My daughter would watch silently as I jumped off my wooden stool, often dropping my clean sheets or diapers in the mud. It did not help that M. Grenier was seeding the whole property. I would make a grab for my daughter and race for the safety of the screened-in porch attached to our little apartment.

At dusk it was safe to venture outdoors as the bees were safely tucked away in their little honeycombs. "Mais Madame Doyle, je vous assures que nos abeilles sont tres amiable." He almost burst into tears when we called the moving van.

If I'm not mistaken, <u>The Inspector General's House</u> came along about this time in our family history. The "General" usually made his rounds around 7 p.m., just when I was getting my little girl ready for bed. Of course, the kitchen was chaotic.

Our landlord had scraped his fingers to the bone for 40 years to buy his dream apartment, and we were in it. In physical appearance, M. Lavoie looked like three days of rainy weather. He went from room to room doing the Duncan Type test with his fingers above doorways and windows, murmuring into his beard about "les femmes Anglaises, mon Dieu, ells so paresseuses." Heaven only knows what he said about French Canadian women. It wouldn't be complimentary either!

A loud moan would accompany the sight of a cracked tile in the bathroom. They were cheapies and my daughter happened to be a curious child. I'd sit and watch her splash water and try to catch the soap bubbles. Eventually the water worked its' way in behind the few tiles. Her little finger marks in the hallway walls sent M. Lavoie into paroxysms of despair.

At the end of the inspection, I'd lead Mr. Inspector General to a kitchen chair. He mopped the sweat from his brow, blew violently into a huge red hankie, and took copious notes on the state of the rooms and went his way ... until the next month. Oh yes, he *never* forgot to pick up his rent cheque.

I am convinced that <u>The Snake House </u>is one of the most bizarre homes we ever owned. It was on Carletta Drive in Mississauga, Ontario. It was a great buy because no one else wanted the work involved in renovating it.
Close your eyes for a minute to imagine the wildest jungle scene you are able to conjure up ... like slithering vines with giant leaves, enormous drooping sunflowers of deep purple,

as well as hot pink and bright orange nestlings in amongst chartreuse green foliage. Now I suggest you take this jungle nightmare out of your mind and glue it all over kitchen walls, doors, window sills and cupboards. The interior decorating in the rest of the house matched the kitchen, purple ceilings, chocolate brown walls and a violent red in the master bedroom.

There were no locks or doorknobs to be found. The snow blew in and left drifts of snow in the hallway. Of course little critters walked in and made themselves comfortable. We had "visitors" for weeks after we moved in.

By mid-March we had the house redecorated with the efforts of our own aching backs. I couldn't wait to get out back and sit under that enormous apple tree that spread out the width of the property. In April, the snow disappeared and I had to face up to still another new reality.

You see two million apples fell annually for this apple tree. 99.9% of these apples fell to the ground. After eight years of apple droppings, you build up a pretty good ground cover of, well ... mush. We were getting down to the flower beds when ... moving vans rolled in.

Some homes are built on the bedrocks and others, it appears, are built on giant onion patches that thrive on sand and ants, which leads me into describing <u>The Ant House</u> in Danvers, Massachusetts, USA.

It was a radiant heated house and there were three hundred other families in our sub-division all using radiating heat – and ants together. There was no basement, so heating consisted of a furnace next to the kitchen stove. I am convinced that the heat radiated onto the ground underneath this heat box which had all the ants within a quarter of a mile radius simply jumping for joy. The ants came, saw, and conquered. Literally thousands of them were *everywhere.*

It was the darn scouts that almost *done me in.* Yes, ants have *scouts* who go on dangerous missions (like the sugar bowl and the butter dish) and then they push up their little antenna and *bleep*, *bleep* a short code message back to Mission Control. Just when you think you've got them, they scamper back into the wood work before you can get even one squirt of Raid out of the can.

Every family has ants. However, no one talked about them. Being a foreigner and unfamiliar with Yankee New England ways, I accidentally blurted it out one day when "the girls" were having coffee with me. What followed was like a group encounter blow-up. Some cried and hissed witch-like concoctions they'd developed over the years to rid themselves of the dreaded monsters.

We held our noses as we painted linseed ground Sulphur with molasses as well as cod liver oil all over wood work, doors and any ant escape hatches we could find. I was working on concoction #7 when I got the word ... and off we were, back to Canada. I had to ask myself what mysterious haunts lay ahead. As right as rain, they were always sure to come.

Adventures in the Silver Streak: Allan gets his Christmas wish

It was a radical departure on our part to break with tradition and head south to celebrate our 1974 Christmas. That *is* what we did and it wasn't very easy to try and satisfy the needs of two children under eight years of age, as well as two teenagers in so far as Christmas wishes were concerned.

We had, on the plus side, the best car of our married lives thanks to the St. Lawrence car policy for all of its senior managers. Our brand new Chevrolet Caprice (air conditioned) was a silver colour. Mo and Michael, by the way, were celebrating their Christmas together in Canada.

The six of us set out for Florida on December 21st. We tried to beat a big snow storm but holed up in Toronto for a day and night. Then we made a beeline for the I-75. We were equipped with a c.b. radio which enabled us to keep track of the U.S. smokies (police) along the way. The loyal troupe of cars also heading south kept us abreast of any possible interventions in the form of speeding tickets. There would be "horn honking" as we passed our travellin' buddies. For some inexplicable reason, our car was dubbed *The Silver Streak.*

It seemed like an eternity by the time we arrived in Atlanta, Georgia. Warm, muggy and flowers in bloom, we stopped at a large mall and went straight to the department store – Christmas decoration section. It didn't take long to find what we were looking for: a huge pine tree, smelling like the real ones, yet folded up. The clincher was the half-price ticket. Since it was a $90.00 item we immediately got the eye and interest of the floor manager. He turned on the charm and offered to throw in ornaments, tinsel and other decorations as a bonus.   It was a done deal, and dad had his wallet out all ready to part with his U.S. bucks.

We hadn't reckoned on the concerns expressed by a little red-headed four year old of ours: "You promised me a *real* tree," he whimpered. We whirled around in our seat, and there was Allan, his hands on his hips, and if looks could have killed we would have passed on. We knelt down, we two parents, on either side of Allan and patiently explained about the snow storm and it detaining us. We believed that there would not be time to buy a real tree anywhere in Florida on December 24th.

Allan dug in his heels. His voice took on a stronger tone. "Santa won't come if we don't have a real tree. I want one," he bellowed. The floor manager, now seeing his artificial tree sale slipping through his fingers knelt down on the floor between the two perspiring parents. "Son, please bend over to this branch. Smell the sweet perfumes of the pine forest. Not even Santa can tell the difference. This tree is as good as any tree you'll find in the forest," he concluded. Al was having none of our pleading and soliloquies. He stamped his four year old foot and said, "I want a *real* tree." We knew when we were beaten so we bid a sad adieu to the dejected manager.

Now it was Operation Real Christmas Tree. Mile after mile we drove, all six of us peering through windows for a glimpse of a real tree. All we saw were bare, empty spaces on

Christmas tree lots that said boldly, "no more trees left" on cardboard signs.

We had to get gas before we hit Jacksonville, Florida and we stopped at a garage hook-up in the middle of nowhere. All of a sudden Allan let out a wild whoop. "There it is!" he shouted triumphantly. "I see my tree over on the other side of the garage!" Dad walked over and lifted up a tree that had been left leaning on the outside wall. A sorrier sight one did never see. It was a Charlie Brown replica; thin, wispy, sickly-looking branches, with a permanent lean in the left direction. The top had been broken off completely.

The mechanic could see Al jumping for joy. It was clearly evident that all caution had been thrown to the winds, and little hope remained of a bargain deal being offered for the second time in the same day. "So, how much do you want for me to take this thing off your hands?" Dad carefully ventured. Knowing desperation in a man's eye when he saw it, the mechanic's response was crisp and cool. "Eleven bucks," he stated. Every cent seemed way overboard.

Taking another glance at Allan's radiant face, Dad heaved a sigh and paid up.

We found some thick emergency rope in the trunk and strapped The Real Tree on the top of The Silver Streak. Horn honks greeted us along the way as travellin' buddies from far and near spotted the wispy green tree on our car roof. As we drove on, we could sense the laughter all around us, and we buckled under looks of wonder that seemed to say, "Calling Silver Streak from Canada – what's happening here today to you guys? Did you pick up a Charlie Brown tree along the way?" The lanes around us felt like they opened up and we became the great tease with our green purchase perched atop our crown.

At last we arrived at our condo beach rental in New Smyrna Beach. We picked up decorative balls, lights and a garland at a supermarket, and borrowed a pail from the janitor. We raced for the shore, and Allan and John filled the pail up with warm sand to house the sapling. Shortly our "bit of green" was tenderly placed in the pail of sand, with the left leaning side resting against the wall lest it topple over.

When the mission was accomplished and the green wish was bedecked with tiny balls, two strings of lights, thick garland woven in and out, and abundant foil tinsel sprinkled from each tiny branch, it was truly a tree transformed. The look on Allan's face made it all worthwhile. "Now I know Santa will come tonight," he said, face all aglow. Sure enough, Al was right.

A Day in the Life of Ivan Katz

This true story was written on September 26, 1973 at Manoir Ste. Castin in Quebec where we had our new home at the time.

Katz entered our lives on a bright sunny day at Lac Beauport, twenty miles from Quebec City. My spouse and I decided we would take a half-day holiday and meander around the place. Mr. Katz's canoe overturned and we raced together to drag him in, as he was, fortunately for all of us concerned, very close to shore. Despite our pleas to the contrary, Katz insisted that we join him for a drink on the terrace. He and his wife were American guests at the posh Manoir Ste. Castin for two weeks.

We carefully explained that we had left our three children home with a babysitter, and that we were only sightseeing for a few hours. Katz suddenly invented all kinds of plans for us, and HE was included in all of them! It was a struggle, but we finally got away. Almost, that is.

We figured that renting a boat would be the safest escape route. Katz followed suit. We hid behind an island. Katz's cheery, "hi there folks," a few minutes later told us we weren't very good at our tactics to disappear! The lake isn't that big and you can't really go around and around in circles forever.

We finally came to face the music. Katz was nice; one simply couldn't dislike him. His warm brown eyes, wide smile and enthusiasm crippled a person's hate glands. The biggest obstacle to continued friendship was that he took over. I mean body and soul. Our big problem lay in getting rid of him … politely. When I get desperate, I get crazy ideas, like the horseback riding suggestion that I made to escape Katz's clutches. It didn't work you know.
Katz purred like a kitten when he heard mention of … HORSES ! We immediately received, in rapid-fire order, a complete list of hunting and riding clubs of which he frequented. Katz became misty-eyed recalling those times of hunting and riding under the stars at a Texas riding ranch. I could see him in my mind's eye, going off to dreamland with a mink throw to keep his toes warm, while a bottle of Pouilly-Fuisse was cooling in a nearby steam.

I ventured a timid comment at this point to the effect of Mr. Katz should not be expecting too much of *this* particular riding stable. "It's only a small farm, you know," I ventured. Katz's smile only broadened and he showed even more of his pearly-whites.

We pulled up in front of a dilapidated group of buildings about a mile from the Manoir. Katz marched over to the barn. He spoke with firmness and authority to the tall, gangly boys, "je veux un cheval avec d'esprit, ye boys, ye boys." Katz spoke to the taller "boy," dressed in faded jeans, a man with a jaw slackened by improperly fitting dentures. The man looked at Katz, studying him from the top of his coiffed head, monogrammed beige tailored polo shirt, deep brown riding jodhpurs, down to his gleaming high riding boots. A riding crop completed the outfit. The "boys" exchanged hysterical glances and entered the stables to look over their "stock."

The stock consisted of five worn-out nags ready for the first call from the nearest glue factory. Katz's smile faded momentarily, his glance indicating that there wouldn't be much of that *esprit* he had asked for from the stable boys. Ah, well, sugar cubes could be the answer! Katz had brought along a big bag of them. "That ought to fire him up a little," he confided to me.

As for me, I told the cow hand that I was strictly a "une debutante," and I wanted an animal as slow as cold molasses, and if at all possible, as close to the ground as a dachshund. My response drew forth a big giggle from the guys as they answered, "oui Madame, bien sure."

Old Iron Pants sauntered over to me, and I quivered in my boots, or to be truthful, my two inch heeled shoes. The old nag they gave me looked as if she could plough every field in the province. She gave a look that sent shivers up my back. After three tries I finally got on, and the reins were put in my already sweaty hands. All the while Katz was murmuring endearments, such as "you can do it honey," and "there you go. Keep that back straight as a rod now. Let that horse know who's boss." I let go of my death grip on the reins for a few brief seconds to turn and glare at Mr. Katz. "SHE KNOWS WHO'S BOSS," I retorted, 'AND IT'S CERTAINLY NOT ME."

We went toward the so-called trail, which was a two-foot wide muddy trough in dense bush. The "guides" threw snickering glances from time to time at our friend Katz, who wore a rather woebegone expression on his face.

We rounded a thicket of bushes at this point, and things did look brighter. There was a running brook, old farm houses, and a sprinkling of magnificent evergreen trees. "Oh Honey," Katz called out, "do try to follow more closely behind me. I like to marvel with someone at the feasts that Mother Nature offers us." His arms spread out expansively. "Look yonder, my dear, at these giant trees. People in the southwest of the United States would give a FORTUNE to have a tree like this in their back yard." He then waited for me to catch up, and in a conspiratorial whisper stated that he knew just what would lift my sagging spirits.

"Why look," Katz exclaimed, 'THAT'S NO WAY TO MAKE A HORSE WOMAN OUT OF YOU! YOU HAVE *GOT* TO FEEL THE WIND CARRESS YOUR FACE, HEAR THE POUNDING OF HOOVES, TREES AND SKY HURTLING PAST YOU."

Suddenly, Katz dealt a smart smack on the right flank of my horse with his riding crop. Iron Pants reared up, baring her teeth at this indignity, nostrils flaring and took off into the bush as if pursued by a horde of wasps attacking from the rear.

I don't recall much about the next few minutes as everything was a blur. I have only a vague recollection of Katz galloping behind me shouting at the top of his lungs, "VUNDEBAR AT LAST. YOU'VE DONE IT!" YOU ARE REALLY RIDING NOW LIKE A PRO." My sunglasses flew off, and I threw caution to the winds. I threw my arms around the brute's neck and hung on for dear life. Out of nothing else except sheer terror, I dug in my two inch heels into Old Iron Pants' flanks. SHE THOUGHT THAT I MEANT FOR HER TO SPEED UP, AND READILY COMPLIED. Two miles later, we came to the fence, at which time horse and rider parted company. I hurriedly declined Katz's dinner invitation on behalf of the two of us.

To this day, I confess that I have avoided riding stables as I would an epidemic of Bubonic plague.

Sophie: Queen for a day

In 1996, I changed my lifestyle, and it was a complete change after 43 years. There is *nothing* like "Home Sweet Home" for me. I was raised in two homes – one on a farm at Williams Point, in the country of Antigonish, Nova Scotia. Following that, we moved into the *town* of Antigonish.

"That is where you will receive the best education anywhere in Canada," my teacher-Mom told us. Indeed to me she was right on the money: it suited my Christian background as well as my parent's high-level dreams for all their children.

My move to Preston in Cambridge, Ontario in 1996 was a dream come true for me. For one thing, my youngest son Allan was already residing in Preston, and it reminded me of a "larger" Antigonish!

I say that with a smile, because my birth town was a tiny place... *period*. The Grand River was in full steam ahead, and happened to be in that state of mind when I began to house-hunt. One son tried his best to show me a brand new apartment building with elevators, extra services and also, a stone's throw from the Grand River. I turned them all down.

My thoughts go back to the day when I first set eyes upon Sophie. We both walked out of our homes simultaneously – two houses apart. I was "the new neighbour" who was "in town" one week. I *did* see a few curtains flick nervously when I came and went to my car.

I had supreme confidence in *them* before I moved in: the former owners were the pariah's of this 20,000 population community, known as Preston. That is because their manners left much to be desired: their dog left waste on a neighbour's property and … and … they had a small sex shop just off King Street! (the main street, specifically).

Sophie was adorable, in every way: 4ft, 10 inches – petite (size 2) and loved clothes. On the day we met in 1998 (when I bought my home), Sophie was irresistible, the last of a family of eight girls. "My poor father prayed for a son but it never happened," she told me.

Sophie explained that she "was the closest thing to being a boy because I had so much spunk. My behind is so flat because of that too. I would get a smart smack on my bottom when I spoke out of turn or stole the last piece of cake 'from my elders.'" Sophie further indicated that "the meanest grandma in the world" made it "nearly impossible" for her to "keep her slate clean" at church attendance. Sophie felt she needed to bow her head longer due to the pile-up of sins she needed to account for, especially if she missed her Lutheran service.

Everyone loved Sophie on my street. That was due to the fact that Sophie was the last to be alive in her overly-large home. Sophie "was not a spender at all" and received a pension "from The Big Boys" in Ottawa.

There were two other impediments to her living "very much longer ... even though I want to do so very much." Sophie explained that "her milk-drinking habits of more than 80 plus years" were the reason she could "manage the stairs, walk up the hill to Hamilton Street, and go to the grocery store where canned goods are all the best and cheapest."

I asked Sophie why she didn't prefer fresh foods and I offered to take her in my car. "No, no Loretta, that is because my canned goods are for the poor. I take a bag each Sunday and if I miss, every once in a while, I still put the missed church envelope "in the basket." Without asking, she supplied the following belief system: "my sisters and I knew what it is like to be hungry during the dirty thirties. That's what we called it inside our home. My Papa had no work, and everyone else *exceptin'* those rich jewelry stores were *still* goin' strong."

"One sister left home to be a nurse and even saw a Royal family visit at her hospital. Oh, how our eyes were bulging' big that night when we got the whole story," Sophie told me. "Then three years later a sad event hit the family all at once." Sophie continued. "You see my sister married and that was good. The sad thing was she didn't actually *live* here much anymore."

The neighbours all around both Sophie and I were most protective. Sometimes, we neighbours, caused trouble for ourselves too. There was one occasion when policeman Mike on our street, did too. I met Sophie's "other" relatives on one occasion a year after I was in my home. They appeared controlling and mean-spirited to me. I kept my peace however, while in their company after my first introductions. Then one day Sophie phoned saying she "missed a step and her back was hurting badly." I suggested I come over and perhaps it would be wise to call her M.D. or a family member.

Sophie immediately called out, "Not those mean ladies who want my money!" I did go over and suggested it would *still* be helpful if she saw a medical doctor or even a nurse at the clinic two streets away. She insisted her electric back support would "do the trick" but it was broken.

I stayed the afternoon with Sophie, bringing chamomile tea bags, tiny shortbreads *after* chicken noodle soup, and somehow she was "all better." Then the "mean sisters" burst in on Sophie. They were furious that "some neighbour with no family connections" had interfered. "Poor Sophie:" She was, I thought, caught between a rock and a hard place... She "lost her temper and really gave it to them," and "to leave her alone." "I told you Loretta, that's why my behind is so flat." It was all I could do, to keep from bursting into laughter as well as *shout out a few Hallelujahs!*

The policeman Mike, a dear man, intervened on Sophie's behalf as well. "He knows business as well as keeping peace around the town," Sophie said. I readily agreed.

A week later, Sophie let me know over her picket fence that "Mike got the dickens from his boss." I asked what happened. "It turned out," Sophie recounted, as a tear or two trickled down her cheeks, "that my mean relatives reported him." "I knew it," Sophie said, with a triumphant ring in her voice, "they were goin' into my bank stuff I buried down-deep-and-low in my trunk." My heart ached for this dear precious friend and neighbour.

Sophie phoned to say her old fridge had "kicked the bucket." I asked for an interpretation: "my milk is sour, and so I opened up a can of spam" – which I thought was quite clever of her. My neighbours Marion and Phil were similar friends to Mike and his wife Marion: first class couple in that they minded their own business, and yet were at your door if help was needed.

Phil declared Sophie's 40 year old fridge "dead as a door nail." He suspected that it had "been dying a silent death for some months" and Sophie wasn't able to detect it. Of course one would expect "the mean sisters" to object when Phil went out immediately and purchased a smaller fridge and installed it the same day. He made sure to make a copy of Sophie's receipt as well.

Each time a family member came to visit me, I made sure Clare (sister) met Sophie, along with Gerald (brother). Every single person, with the exception of *her* family, "fell in love" with

Sophie as she was ... *incorruptible.* It was Sophie's custom to boast about her trip to Germany one fine summer. She praised her travels to the skies: and went once on a tour all through towns and cities. Being kind to all who met and loved her and came to her home, Sophie would show her "gift of Jesus" that was hung in the hall foyer for all eyes to see once they were inside. And the final sentence all visitors heard was always the same: "This image was a gift. "Jesus" was hung in the hall foyer for all eyes to see once they were inside. It was her piece de resistance. It was ALWAYS a terrific moment for me to *restrain* myself ... but more importantly, my visitors. The photo was ... Martin Luther! Sophie was stone deaf in one ear from a bad fall. Luckily, she missed the error entirely.

There is one other tender story about my friend Sophie that would be shameful to pass over: In our quiet summer moments together, on her wooden swing, dear unbelievable Sophie told me the family secret. I thought that it would be "better left unsaid," since I was "not family" and *the mean sisters* would be upset to know, if the secret became known. I assured Sophie I was not one to tell tales out of school due to my parent's upbringing.

My Daddy told me "there is *inside* talk, and it is *not* for sale to anyone except our family. The *outside* talk is kind, but hopefully funny or happy talk to *share.*" I confess having gotten into "trouble" once, through innocence rather than sinfulness. In my school days, Mother St. Miriam told me to tell my parents to order a new school uniform. My father examined my uniform closely and declared it was "still good to wear." He added a sentence, which at 9 years of age, I didn't understand, was to be placed in the *inside* category.

I came home from school at the end of the day from Mount St. Bernard College. I explained to my dad, who always read the newspapers first, was involved in his reading period, and ignored my first statement. I repeated it louder, expecting a smiling response. Instead there was a roar, and he lifted himself upright from his usual-head-of-the-table chair and said "You what? You told that Reverend Mother that I said she was full of PRUNES?!"

Shocked to hear him, dear Daddy, who brought home bags of candy to each of us, according to our desires, needed an answer. My voice was low and quiet. "Well Daddy, *she* asked me. I *thought* you wanted me to *give her an answer* about my *uniform.*" Naturally, he quieted down, put his arm around me, and told me what The Foley Family Method was from that day on.

Dear Sophie had an adoring father as well. Her "secret" fell from her lips quickly and with spirit. "My grandma hated my Papa, who did so much want his family to be well-off and safe. She made fun of my Papa and even held back a cookie for him when me and my sisters made a visit to her big house at Christmas time. Mamma was the one who said we *had* to go and visit with a gift. We didn't want to, and she would say, "What would Jesus say?" We would all walk together to her house and "put on our best behavior" "as Mama taught us to love all in the world."

"My Papa," she told me, "was sad to not have a proper job during *the Big Decession*" (Sophie could not pronounce the word "Recession"). He would buy pieces of wood from a lumber yard that had marks on them. A yard worker saw a joyful look in Papa's eyes and drove him home in his truck, even though the piece of wood stuck out like a sore thumb and needed two red handkerchiefs to warn people of danger. All eight children sat at the table too.

Now to the big secret: Papa "liked *a nip or two of the rum*, when he was down and out, picking up beer/pop bottles off the railway tracks." "He got 0.5 cents per bottle," Sophie proudly told me, as if it were a badge of honour. Her Papa did not always attend church like her mother did when she was able to do so. "Mama served so many hours for her eight girls. She never once thought of herself."

On Sundays, two pennies would usually be put in each of the girls' hands. They were to put the coins into the church basket that was passed around for those in need. The canned goods came later when Sophie was hired at the Savage Shoe Factory in Preston. It was a glorious day for all! One Sunday, the sisters deposited their pennies as usual. Sophie had sharp eyes and noticed the giggles from three wealthy girls across the aisle. "It was a 'humiliation' for our family with a proud name of 'Shultz,'" claimed Sophie. She told her father about it, and with her fiery spirit told him "one day I will be the one to have $$$ saved from my new job." Indeed, it came true five years later when the rich girls had no work.

To cheer Sophie up, Papa suggested to her that she go and pick her some "lavenders," as he called them. "They will all be pouring out of the earth now. Go get me a good-sized basket to load up a big bunch from our favourite patch close to the evergreens that keep them nice and moist. They will last a long time dear," he said to Sophie. Sophie told me she wiped away her tears and ran to the place under the old sink, where she was to find the biggest and strongest wicker basket. There were hugs for all who were home. Mama said, "Now be careful along that railway track and we will all wait supper for you."

Hours passed and Papa did not return. Finally, an M.D. came by the house. He had a sad story to relate about "dear Papa" who was "going deaf" earlier than was usual. The lavender flowers were as moist in the wicker basket as they were in the ground. "The train was going so fast around the turn, no brakes on this earth could have stopped and saved this fine family's man," the M.D. stated.
Sophie told me why her garden is filled with "lavenders" because she took the basketful of her father's. It was so moist and it was warm, as well as full of nutrients from "the good earth."

These 'dear lavenders' were so kind and generous to gardens such as mine. My earth opened up to their arms, to Sophie's lavenders, because we each needed new soil and a blossom to grow in a brand new garden such as mine.

To this day, I look out and see my own 'dear lavenders' spawned by Sophie's precious ones from her father.

It was a sad day when I received a call from Sophie to say she had a stroke in her home after falling down some of the long stairway. She was hospitalized, and she recovered. The neighbours visited her and rejoiced. Her savings and investments were still hers and she grew plump in the nursing home named Sunnyside. At Sunnyside, she continued to brighten other resident's lives for the good number of years left to her. There is a quote I heard as a young child: "He/she laughs best, who laughs last." Sophie is laughing to her heart's content.

Williams Point

In July 1996, I read a book about life in the country (Boulton), and it took me back, as always, to Williams Point, and as well to the early days at the cottage.

We all learned a lot together at the cottage. A picture that comes to mind was me sitting in a pile of sawdust in a corner, nursing baby Allan and watching dad hammer and cut and grind screws into this and that. We were, remember, in an A- frame building, with only the roof, sides, and nothing inside but the beams. So we built gradually and lived in the mess at the same time.

There is another scene in my head: my family -- Mike, Allan, John and Brian all sitting on the old dock, which was our original "first dock" and all of them are looking towards the island. I took a picture of that as I loved the quiet togetherness: no rowdiness or horsing around, just sitting together peacefully. Mike got the "joe jobs" and would help make "pieces" of cement so that the job could be completed section by section over many years.

As I look back, I doubt that there was any time in our lives when we had so many happy hours as we did in those days. Nickels were earned from carrying water up from the lake because we had no running water. I helped too, and oh, how I hated that job! There were so many tree roots sticking out of the ground as well as those blinking rocks!

Of interest too, was the number of times my recipes called for an item I did not have: innovation was the order of the day. Dad's electric cattle prod to heat the bath water was a riot. No one was allowed to go near it in case they would be zapped.

The lake water was your bathtub and mine too. Ron found it too cool for the most part. He'd spend an hour or two in the tub at night, and he built a bookstand that extended across the tub. I used to tease him he'd be a prune at the end of the evening following his nightly reading.

The fires down at the water's edge were wonderful. I've always been addicted to outdoor fires for as long as I can remember. Firesides are magical, and no fire is ever the same as another. Oh yes, the kids drove us crazy: poking at the embers, sneaking tiny sticks in at the bottom of the fire box to see if sparks would dance up in the black night. Oh yes, we'd yell out, "don't burn yourselves for God sakes," and Allan, the hunter for "bitch" bark pieces loved to throw them on for a hot burst. We'd have buckets of water ready in case the fire grew out of control and start to spread up the hill.

We burnt so many old boards and debris from Don Anderson's first carpentry attempts. Never mind – I'm grateful to the Andersons because they sold us their dreams for a very low price – what they paid to the cent. The work involved was simply too much for them. We were gluttons for punishment and I can recall cleaning out the little leaches as one of the most unsavory jobs of all. Clean them out we did. Once the rotten leaves were raked out along with the rotten branches and driftwood on the lake bottom, as well as the rocks moved into form for the old dock, the leaches vacated our premises forever.

Leroy Nilmo had an idea to barge in sand for the shoreline. Yes it was bought and dumped at Anderson's and a barge was built by his sons. We paid for part and it was shoveled on at Anderson's by a fellow from Oshawa, and then shoveled into Nilmo's shoreline and ours. It looked to me like a losing battle: as fast as we'd shovel it in it seemed as if a wave would prance in and take the shovelful back out!

Not much remains of our sandy shoreline and today we'd be fined mega bucks by the forestry department if we touched the shoreline and they were aware of it. Ron had the road put in down to the waters' edge, a grace given to grandpapa, or those unable to get down to get in water! Yes it was sneaky but at least Grandpapa was of some positive "value" to all of us. As Ron and I predicted when all your moans, groans and angry statements about rape of the land were at their most vocal, nature filled in the holes, nooks and crannies.

I love the maple and cedar "bunches" that have replaced the old pine trees at the bottom of the hill on Nilmo's side. The pine trees that are standing now are *it* for awhile. I'd rather have many more deciduous trees come in their place.

When I went back to the cottage after some weekends away, it was great to find the plastering was done, painting complete. It was quite something to see the finished product after a 25 year wait. There were a few finishing touches but really it was most attractive. The trick was to stop thinking work equals cottage; cottage equals work and ... ***enjoy*** the fruits of our labours! I made a promise to myself that fun comes first there from then on.

I figure there will come a day, and a lot sooner than one thinks, that the hill will be hell to climb, the lake swim-to-island for me that I love now, will be too much of a task. These "golden" years do have many limitations. Being grateful for function in all areas – physical, mental, emotional and spiritual comes to mind. I truly do not feel older in my head; it is the same as when I was 25. However, the spirit is willing, the flesh is weak.

Gratitude

Every single day is a blessing. Freedom is the name of the game I love to play: attending theatrical performances, reading new and fascinating books, starting an exercise program where I can do water aerobics in a warm pool.

In short, I embrace change, looking expectantly to the next fun or fascinating surprise. Take for example last week. I had a phone call from my eldest son, Brian. He teaches one half of his academic day at Humber College and in the afternoon, he does professional counselling with students.

Brian left a message that had an enticing suggestion: "Hi Mom, it's me, Brian. I have an all-clear P.M. today. Can I come to your home, carrying parts of a dinner and we'll put on our aprons and cut the veggies? I'll slice the pork and we'll do a stir-fry." Talk about fun! We laughed and went back into family history ... and were closer than I can remember as a mother and son.

My youngest son Allan is completing a doctoral thesis in Art History from Princeton University. Usually the youngest of a large family of five children is either a "playboy" or .... what Al is, a scholar who puts his nose to the grindstone seven days a week. There is no T.V., no social activities in general and it's all about research and one more journal, hoping for a sentence or two of new and vital information on an artist who lived more than 100 years ago. Mostly the long hours spent do not discover a *eureka moment*," as did Archimedes, the Greek philosopher, sitting in his bath tub.

I have mentioned earlier that I thoroughly embrace change: it comes like an inner joy, identical to what my daddy brought when he would return home after work with seven tiny unopened bags of penny-store candies for his children. Al was asked to live in the U.S. for two to three weeks at a time, to live like royalty in a wealthy home, by a fine couple who are given an opportunity to "get away" in the sun. I hold my breath to share the next news with you: Al is to "cat sit" for a foundling stray cat, now grown to maturity.

Al is free to use this home, pool and the comforts of extreme wealth. His only task, at 50.00 U.S. dollars daily, is to "house sit" for Tabi. He is to see to her diet and emotional well-being and yes, make up her bedspread. After all, a cat needs a tidy room which has a down-filled pillow.

The new century surely brings additional stress; we as persons either jump into a new millennium or the opposite. I personally have always embraced changes in my life. One experiences an internal feeling of excitement with a sort of "off with the old – on with the new" sentiment.

Since the birth of 2001, I am able to look back in my journal with a deep sense of thankfulness, and know beyond a shadow of a doubt that overall, my life is going FORWARD. Yes, there were acquaintances who said with raised eyebrows, "why, *why* are you going back to school again? Or why are you involved in a memoirs class?" Those dear classmates responded with a resounding "*yipes*" reaction upon hearing me say, "I love it" or "my brain gets exercise" or "I met some lady whose company I will enjoy for many years to come."

Secretly, these years have turned out to be the best years of my life; single once again, and comfortable financially. Being a good manager has helped me remarkably all of my life. As the years quicken, my spirit finds perpetual strength and refreshment from a faith and purpose conferred on me since my earliest days with my beloved parents. They have planted the tiniest seeds of courage, kernels of a fertile life for which I remain forever grateful.

About the Author

Loretta won her first award in grade two for her own account of the story of Pinocchio. In her later years, Loretta was compelled to tell her story through Segments & Slices, a local writing group.

Loretta was born in Antigonish, Nova Scotia in Canada and has loved the Atlantic Ocean for as long as she can remember.

Her mother, Mary Ann MacDonald, was the "mainstream" of their family, and spoke fluent Gaelic at home in her native Cape Breton. Mary Ann became an elementary school teacher who "went west" with her older sister at the end of 1917-1918. She taught her children that *to be true to oneself* was paramount.

Loretta's father, Michael Joseph Foley was born in Prince Edward Island, and worked in the coal mines. He was devoted to his family, despite losing his own mother in childbirth. His father was a tailor and a deeply religious man.

Loretta was a natural-born reader, winning prizes every year. She loved the land around her that had wild roses and every possible tree. The landscape enticed her to fall in love with her east coast world, especially the ocean. Growing up in a family of five girls and two boys, they were introduced to large libraries early on. The family went to operatic plays in her Catholic Church. Sports and fresh air were immensely important to one and all.

Loretta's parents believed strongly in a good education for boys and girls alike. A convent of nuns, many with PhD's, moved from Quebec to the College of Mount St. Bernard and educated the girls. The nuns instilled a love for music in Loretta which remains to this day. Just a few days before graduation when Loretta was awarded a Governor General's medal for her studies, her beloved mother passed away. Loretta cried for days at the immense loss in her life and became a surrogate mother to her sisters.

In spite of her profound loss, Loretta's father appealed to her to pursue education at St. Francis Xavier University in Antigonish, Nova Scotia. Following this Loretta furthered her studies in psychiatric social work at McGill

University in Montreal, Quebec, and completed her internship.

Loretta was pleased to assume the daunting task of serving female inmates as the first social worker at Kingston Prison for Women in Kingston, Ontario. As a mother to five children, Loretta was in her 40's when she decided to return to school and pursue a Masters of Social Work degree at Carleton University in Ottawa. Loretta opened an extremely successful private practice in the field of family health in Northern Ontario, serving as the only trained therapist in the region.

Today Loretta enjoys her retirement years and resides in the Preston area of Cambridge, Ontario. Loretta enjoys taking a stroll along the Grand River, dancing in her living room, and meeting up monthly with good friends from her church. Twice weekly she can be found at the William E. Paulter 50+ Recreation Centre, exercising. When sharing a pot of tea with friends and family alike, Loretta can be counted on to ask, "And what is the *best* thing that happened to you this week?"

Loretta's fondest memories include spending time at the family cottage in Bolton, Ontario and travelling overseas to Israel with a fifty-four unit group.